Dear Uncle
William,
Merry X-mas 2007
Love Philly X

kings of comedy

Johnny Acton
and
Paul Webb

Main Street
A division of Sterling Publishin
New York

D0257946

10 9 8 7 6 5 4 3 2 1

Library of Congress Cataloging-in-Publication Data Available

Published by Main Street, a division of Sterling Publishing Co., Inc.
387 Park Avenue South, New York, NY 10016

First Published in Great Britain in 2005 by
Think Publishing
The Pall Mall Deposit
124-128 Barlby Road, London W10 6BL
www.think-books.com

Text © Think Publishing and GCAP Media plc 2005
Design and layout © Think Publishing and GCAP Media plc 2005
The moral rights of the author have been asserted.

Written by Johnny Acton and Paul Webb
Edited by Emma Jones
The *Kings of Comedy* team: Christopher Bennett, James Collins, Rica Dearman,
Rhiannon Guy, Matt Packer, Mark Searle, Lou Millward Tait and Suzi Williams

Distributed in Canada by Sterling Publishing
c/o Canadian Manda Group, 165 Dufferin Street
Toronto, Ontario, Canada M6K 3H6

For information about custom editions, special sales, premium and
corporate purchases, please contact Sterling Special Sales
Department at 800-805-5489 or specialsales@sterlingpub.com.

ISBN-13: 978-1-4027-3675-9
ISBN-10: 1-4027-3675-4

Printed & bound in Singapore by KHL Printing Co.
The publishers and authors have made every effort to ensure the accuracy and currency of
the information in *Kings of Comedy*. Similarly, every effort has been made to contact
copyright holders. We apologize for any unintentional errors or omissions. The publisher
and authors disclaim any liability, loss, injury or damage incurred as a consequence, directly
or indirectly, of the use and application of the contents of this book.
Cover image: The Kobal Collection

Comedy is simply a serious
way of being funny.
Peter Ustinov

WITH THANKS TO

Johnny would like to thank:

Percy, his wife, for her ideas and encouragement

Paul Webb, who wrote a third of the book at short notice

Emma, the editor, for keeping her patience until the final day

Everyone he knows for putting up with his Les Dawson

impressions during the writing of this book

Paul would like to thank:

Sheridan Morley for the use of his library

Nuala Harvey for a fruitful introduction

Emma for inviting me into the book

Johnny ditto

Ben Crystal for wise words of advice

CONTENTS

Funny business

FOR COMEDIANS, WORK *IS* A LAUGHING MATTER

COMEDIANS AND THE CLOTH

**A few top comics have come mighty close
to taking holy orders:**

Dan Aykroyd
expelled from a Jesuit seminary

Lenny Bruce
deserves a (dis)honorable mention
for posing as a priest collecting
money for a leper colony during a
pre-fame spell as
a conman

Julian Clary
was an altar boy and choirboy

Johnny Vegas
attended a seminary twice, from
the ages of 11 to 13 and again
when he was 24, after a
bout of depression

Jackie Mason
trained as a rabbi

Michael Moore
was educated at a
Chicago seminary

Hard work pays off in the future.
Laziness pays off now.

Lugubrious US comedian Steven Wright

DAWN FRENCH – BIG BUSINESS

Although she is better known as, variously, the vicar of Dibley, Jennifer Saunders's comedy partner, when the latter isn't being all *Absolute Fabulous*, and the wife of fellow comedian Lenny Henry, Dawn French is also a very successful businesswoman. Specifically, she is in a partnership which produces women's clothing, spurred on by a passionate belief that the "larger lady" can and should be as stylish as her skinnier sisters (of which she is living proof). In 1991, she formed Sixteen47 with her friend Helen Teague, the company taking its name from the fact that 47% of British females were then thought to be size 16 (US size 14) or larger. The firm had spotted a large hole in the market and has subsequently just got, well, bigger and bigger.

Sometimes failure works out better than success. Tommy Cooper's career is a case in point. Cooper's act was premised on his hopeless ineptitude as a conjuror, yet he began his showbiz career as a serious magician. Or at least he tried to. The problem was that audiences seemed to prefer it when his tricks went wrong.

Cooper made his stage debut at 16 at the staff party of a firm of shipwrights in Kent, where he was serving as an apprentice. He had intended to dazzle his colleagues with feats of conjuring, but unfortunately nerves got the better of him and his act started to unravel. Cards began to drop from his sleeves and handkerchiefs got stuck in hollow tubes. The audience was in hysterics. Cooper ran from the stage in tears, but later it occurred to him that he might have stumbled on something important—at least he'd got a laugh. Perhaps he'd do better to concentrate on that side of things.

On the eve of the Second World War, Cooper enlisted in the Horse Guards. A giant of a man (6 ft 4 in and well over 200 lbs), he excelled at boxing, becoming Army Heavyweight Champion. He was even offered a professional contract, but turned it down as he was hooked on the idea of becoming a performer. The breakthrough came when he successfully auditioned for the regimental concert party, whose job was to keep the troops amused in *It Ain't Half Hot Mum* style. On a posting to Egypt, he picked up the fez that was to become his trademark.

Years later, when established as a comedy legend on the basis of his inability to do magic, Cooper would occasionally throw in a genuinely impressive trick to keep audiences on their toes. One classic example involved a hollow tube going berserk, depositing a bottle of wine whenever it was put down.

> I don't want to achieve immortality through my work. I want to achieve it through not dying.
> Woody Allen

THE PEERLESS MANAGEMENT PHILOSOPHY OF DAVID BRENT

David Brent (Ricky Gervais) is the regional manager of the Slough branch of Wernham Hogg, the stationery firm featured in *The Office*. Brent sees himself as quite the business guru, though his staff think he's an idiot . . .

Avoid employing unlucky people—throw half of the
pile of résumés in the bin without reading them.

If work was so good, the rich would have kept
more of it for themselves.

If you can keep your head when all around you have lost theirs, then you
probably haven't understood the seriousness of the situation.

Never do today that which will become
someone else's responsibility tomorrow.

You don't have to be mad to work here! In fact we
ask you to complete a medical questionnaire to
ensure that you are not.

Process and procedure are the last hiding place of people without the wit
and wisdom to do their job properly.

Eagles may soar high, but weasels don't get sucked into jet engines.

Statistics are like a lamppost to a drunken man—more for leaning on
than illumination.

ZEPPO'S BOMB DEAL

Though not the most prominent of the Marx brothers, Zeppo, the youngest, who tended to play the straight man to his siblings' more colorful characters, arguably had more influence on history than the others combined. During his lifetime he was the holder of two US patents. The first was for an uncoupling device used by Second World War bombers to release their cargoes. Alarmingly, these included the atomic weapons dropped on Hiroshima and Nagasaki. The second, awarded in 1969, was much more benign, being awarded for the invention of a heart monitor to be worn on the wrist like a watch.

THE MANY JOBS OF LAUREL AND HARDY

Stan and Ollie did remarkably well in the job market for a spectacularly clumsy pair operating in Depression-era America. Their résumé includes catastrophic spells as:

Sawmill workers (in *Busy Bodies*)

Piano delivery men
(in *The Music Box*)

Butler/maid (the maid played by Stan)
(in *A Chump at Oxford*)

Medieval servants (in *Fra Diavolo*)

Sailors (in *Two Tars*)

Santa's assistants
(in *March of the Wooden Soldiers*)

Street musicians
(in *You're Darn Tootin'*)

Stable hands (in *Wrong Again*)

Christmas-tree vendors
(in *Big Business*)

> ## Work is the curse of the drinking classes.
> Oscar Wilde

CHAPLIN'S NOT-SO-SILENT DEBUT

Charlie Chaplin's mother was a singer named Hannah Hall who performed in London music halls under the stage name Lilly Harley. When Chaplin was a mere five years old, he showed his star quality by taking over from her when she lost her voice in the middle of a song. Halfway through his own performance, the little boy noticed that the stage was being showered with coins. He stopped singing and announced that to the audience that he would finish the song when he'd gathered up the money. They laughed like drains. Chaplin liked the sound and grew up wanting more.

Sadly, his mother became increasingly mentally unstable and was eventually unable to perform. She was admitted to an asylum when her precocious son was seven. Charlie—like his half-brother, Syd Chaplin (born Sydney Hawkes)—subsequently spent his early life in and out of charity homes and workhouses before joining Fred Karno's touring vaudeville troupe aged 17.

> ## Maybe you'll move to Beverly Hills and we'll be neighbors.
>
> Jack Lemmon's prophetic words to Jay Leno, who worked
> as a chauffeur before he hit the big time
> and was ferrying the star around

FAULTY TOWERS

Whether it was Manuel with his hazy grasp of English or Sybil and Polly letting off steam to compensate for having to work with Basil we will never know, but someone at Fawlty Towers, Torquay's most famous hotel, had a habit of messing with the letters on the signpost. The following all cropped up in the title sequence:

**Farty Towels • Fatty Owls • Warty Towels
Watery Fowls • Flay Otters • Flowery Twats**

DROWNING FOR A LIVING

When W. C. Fields was a teenager (and presumably therefore yet to acquire his trademark bulbous drinker's nose), he had a curious dual job at Fortescue's Pier in Atlantic City. His role was to attract customers to the establishment to increase the chances of them purchasing beer and sandwiches. When Fortescue's was busy, Fields juggled. When business was slow, he pretended to drown.

The second part of the job entailed wading into the sea until neck deep and screaming to be rescued. One of his colleagues would then "save" him, carry him into the bar and deposit him on a barrel. He would then be ostentatiously resuscitated. A large crowd would inevitably assemble to watch the drama, whereupon hawkers would appear offering beer and food.

Fields was paid $10 a week for the dubious privilege of working at Fortescue's, plus all the cake he could eat. During lean spells, he might have to drown himself four or five times a day.

Matthew Perry was a teenage tennis champion
Jo Brand was a psychiatric nurse
Eddie Izzard sold ice cream from a kiosk in Bexhill-on-Sea
Jerry Seinfeld sold jewelry from a cart and worked as
a lightbulb salesman
Billy Connolly worked as a welder and was in the British
Territorial Army Parachute Regiment
Bill Murray was a chestnut salesman
Jim Carrey was a factory janitor
Jennifer Aniston was a waitress
Robin Williams was a street-mime artist
Whoopi Goldberg was a funeral parlor makeup artist

LES DAWSON – RENAISSANCE MAN?

The Manchester-born comedian Les Dawson was a man of many talents. For one thing, as a result of breaking his jaw in a boxing match in his youth, he could "swallow" his nose using his lower lip. For another, he was an accomplished pianist, although this fact would have stretched the credibility of audiences subjected to his deliberately out-of-tune music routines. Before he hit the big time, Dawson played the piano in clubs, and, for one memorable spell, in a Parisian brothel.

Although his humor was gruff, deadpan and sometimes earthy, Dawson was a sensitive man who nursed literary ambitions throughout his career. He was the author of several books—this is what brought him to Paris—and was disappointed that they didn't receive more recognition. He also wrote poetry as a young man, although he kept this activity secret as it sat uncomfortably with the tough environment in which he typically worked as a stand up performer on the working men's club circuit.

In 1967, Dawson won the talent show *Opportunity Knocks*. He went on to become a fixture on British TV, presenting the game show *Blankety Blank* (among many others), on which he greatly endeared himself to viewers with his open scorn for the prizes on offer.

> Because we were a kid act, we traveled at half-fare, despite the fact that we were all around 20. Minnie [the Marx Brothers' mother] insisted we were 13 . . . "That kid of yours is in the dining car smoking a cigar," the conductor told her. "And another one is in the washroom shaving." Minnie shook her head sadly: "They grow so fast!"
>
> Groucho Marx

CARREY CRUCIFIED

Few comedians' careers can have started as inauspiciously as Jim Carrey's. When he was 15, his father took him to a comedy club in Toronto called Yuk Yuk's. Observing that his son was always anxious to perform at home and that the MC was encouraging the audience to take the mike, Carrey Senior encouraged Jim to take up the challenge. The pair hastily cooked up a routine that featured Jim impersonating Jimmy Stewart. It was not a success. The patrons started booing, and owner Mark Breslin decided to put on a record that captured their mood: the crowd scene from *Jesus Christ Superstar*. The main lyric was: "Crucify him!," repeated over and over again. Carrey later recalled the event with a shudder: "They were looking at me like I was from the planet Zeptar." He wouldn't go near another comedy venue for the next two years.

> **Kill my boss? Do I dare live out the American Dream?**
>
> Homer Simpson

Comedy on the couch

SOME JOKERS ARE CRAZY FOR A LIVING, SOME ARE JUST CRAZY

If John Cleese had been less repressed, the world would almost certainly have been deprived of such comedic treats as Basil Fawlty tearing out his hair and the Ministry of Silly Walks. Most of Cleese's best-loved characters were frustrated men who were demonstrably close to the edge, from the long-suffering pet purchaser in the "Dead Parrot" sketch to the punctuality-obsessed headmaster in *Clockwise*. But in the 1980s, Cleese decided that it was time to exorcise the demons that had fueled his special brand of comedy. He embarked on an intensive course of psychotherapy, which led to the publication of two wildly successful self-help books, *Families and How to Survive Them* and *Life and How to Survive It*, both co-authored by his therapist Dr. Robin Skynner.

A pedant could point out that Cleese hasn't exactly lived up to the first title, having been married three times, but his books undoubtedly played a role in reducing the stigma attached to therapy. Unfortunately, as the comedian recognized, the public soon became sick of hearing about him and his shrinkery. They wanted the old Cleese back. He, meanwhile, offered £10,000 to any journalist who chose to write about his work rather than his private life.

Cleese first got involved in therapy in the early 1970s. His marriage to fellow *Fawlty Towers* star and co-writer Connie Booth was on the rails, and he was diagnosed with depression after experiencing psychosomatic flu symptoms in 1973. His third and current wife, Alyce Eichelberger, is— you've guessed it—a psychoanalyst. Cleese says she was "prescribed" by his doctor.

> **My routines come out of total unhappiness.
> My audiences are my group therapy.**
>
> Joan Rivers

Spike Milligan is little known in the US, but in Britain he is rightly hailed as one of the fathers of modern comedy. *The Goon Show*, the radio program which he co-wrote and starred in—alongside Peter Sellers, Harry Secombe and Michael Bentine—was one of Britain's most popular, becoming a major influence on the likes of the Monty Python team. Unfortunately, the demands of churning out an episode a week for several years drove him insane. It compounded the effects of shell-shock sustained during the Second World War and Milligan had a string of nervous breakdowns. He had been manic to begin with; thereafter he was wildly unpredictable and sometimes dangerous.

On one occasion, Milligan broke down the door of his neighbor and fellow Goon, Sellers' flat, brandishing a potato peeler and threatening to kill him. He insulted his employers, calling the BBC "an idiot organization run by idiots for idiots," and shot a teenager who was caught in his garden in the bottom. On the other hand, he was a passionate supporter of various causes, particularly environmentalism and animal rights. (He once attempted to stuff 28 lbs of pasta down the throat of the manager of the food hall at Harrods to enlighten him about the suffering of geese force-fed to make foie gras.)

He seemed to mellow in later years, receiving an honorary knighthood in 2000. On his death in 2002, the then-director general of the "idiot" BBC, Greg Dyke, called Milligan "a comic genius."

After 10 years in therapy, my psychologist told me something very touching; he said: "No hablo Ingles."

Late US stand up Dennis Wolfberg

COMEDIANS AND THEIR DIAGNOSES

Howie Mandel (of *St. Elsewhere* fame) – *obsessive compulsive disorder* (His problem is germs—he cannot bring himself to shake hands and has built a second "sterile" home to retreat to when it all gets too much)

Robin Williams has been described as having "voluntary" *Tourette's syndrome* by Oliver Sacks, the celebrated neurologist and author of *Awakenings*

Jim Carrey – *bipolar disorder* (aka *manic depression*)

Rodney Dangerfield – *bipolar disorder*

Carrie Fisher – *bipolar disorder*

Joan Rivers – *bipolar disorder*

Bill Cosby – *attention deficit disorder (ADD)*

PETER SELLERS – WHO'S HE?

The star of, variously, *The Goon Show*, *Dr. Strangelove or: How I learned to Stop Worrying and Love the Bomb* and the *Pink Panther* films, Peter Sellers had an almost infinite capacity to make other people laugh. Unfortunately, he was a particularly unhappy individual who was frequently horribly abusive to his wives and children.

The child of two vaudeville performers, Sellers was indulged by an overprotective mother. When little Peter pushed his aunt into a lit fireplace, for example, she merely chuckled.

Throughout his life Sellers was given to throwing alarming tantrums in public. His upbringing left him with lousy self-esteem ("I writhe when I see myself on screen," he once admitted) and a profoundly impoverished sense of self. "If you ask me to play myself," he once remarked, "I will not know what to do. I do not know who or what I am." It was perhaps this uncertainty and his lack of a developed adult character to rein him in that allowed Sellers to throw himself so fully into his roles, leading one colleague to describe him as "a receptacle rather than a person."

FREUD ON COMEDY

Sigmund Freud wrote a number of essays on humor. He thought that jokes worked in a similar way to dreams, originating in aggressive or obscene ideas that were unacceptable to the "inner censor" and therefore partly suppressed. By releasing "unacceptable" psychic energy in the disguised form of a joke, the individual concerned was able to restore equilibrium and thereby obtain relief. Members of the audience, meanwhile, would be able to release tension produced by the bottling up of socially unacceptable impulses in the form of laughter. By making a joke, Freud wrote: "one spares oneself the affects to which the situation would naturally give rise and overrides with a jest the possibility of such an emotional display."

Of course, the quickest way to kill a joke is to analyze it, but Freud could on occasion be quite funny. "The great question I have not been able to answer," he once wrote, "despite my 30 years of research into the feminine soul, is: 'What does a woman want?'." He also had a good line for people who teased him about his smoking habit and its supposed phallic significance. "Sometimes," he would say, "a cigar is just a cigar."

Freud's grandson Clement is a popular radio comedian in Britain . . .

THE WRIGHT STUFF

American comic Steven Wright's stage persona, which is alternatively deadpan, neurotic and brain-damaged, certainly implies a degree of familiarity with the world of therapy. In the late 1980s, Wright co-wrote a short film entitled *The Appointments of Dennis Jennings*, starring himself, Rowan Atkinson and Laurie Metcalf, which gave him full scope to vent his subliminal fear of psychiatrists. His character in the film is tormented by his relationship with his shrink (Atkinson), who he imagines is seeing his girlfriend behind his back and entertaining friends with lurid accounts of their therapy sessions. These anxieties turn out to be entirely founded. At the film's end, Wright, driven to distraction, shoots his therapist.

The Appointments of Dennis Jennings won the Academy Award for best short film in 1989. Wright admits that, though it looks mighty handsome on his bookshelf, it feels slightly surreal to own an Oscar.

LARRY DAVID LOSES IT

American comedian Richard Lewis makes much play of his psychological troubles. Mel Brooks once said that he "may just be the Franz Kafka of modern comedy." The originator of the phrase "from Hell" (as in "I had the date from Hell"), Lewis has written a best-selling account of his battle with depression, booze, and drugs entitled *The Other Great Depression*. Indeed, he regards his entire act as a form of therapy, although as much for his audiences as for himself. "I go on a long tour, make people happy they're not me and go home," he explains.

Lewis once persuaded fellow comedian Larry David to visit his shrink in New York. After a few group sessions David had had enough. He stood up in the middle of one and blurted out: "I've had it. I don't want to hear you people. You're not helping me, I can't help you—this is insane." Then he ran out of the house pursued, as Lewis describes it, by 10 neurotics intent on dragging him back. David took refuge in a telephone box, and no amount of persuasion could induce him to leave it until the other patients had left.

Some people just don't want to be helped.

Few comedians have fit the "sad clown" stereotype as closely as Tony Hancock. During the 1950s and 1960s, his star vehicle, *Hancock's Half Hour*, was mandatory listening and then viewing in Britain, but success singularly failed to make him happy. The character he played in the show—an irrepressible, self-important snob—was a long way from likable, but he struck a powerful cord with the British public. Unfortunately, it turned out that he represented the sunnier side of his creator's personality.

As with many members of his profession, alcohol played a major role in Hancock's downfall. Shortly before filming the classic sketch "The Blood Donor," he was involved in a minor car accident and found himself too shaken to learn his lines. The producers resorted to using a teleprompter. This was a fatal mistake; relieved of the responsibility of preparing for his performances, Hancock hit the bottle big time. The biggest victims were his wives. The second, Freddie, made five suicide attempts during their seven-and-a-half-month marriage. On the last occasion, Hancock simply watched as she ate a handful of pills and said: "Make a good job of it because I shan't be calling an ambulance." Amazingly, she didn't hold it against him. "I still believe I was lucky to have married him," she said in an interview 30 years later.

In his later years, Hancock grew increasingly bitter and paranoid, alienating or sacking everyone close to him. In 1968, he committed suicide in Australia, leaving a note which read that "things just went wrong too many times."

> **The prison psychiatrist asked me if I thought sex was dirty. I told him only when it's done right.**
>
> Woody Allen

GETTING ANIMATED ABOUT FRASIER

Each episode of the sitcom devoted to Kelsey Grammer's radio shrink begins with a title sequence of the Seattle skyline "drawing itself." But there are 19 subtle variations . . .

The light at the top of the Space Needle flashes

An elevator rises up said Space Needle

Lights go on in the city's skyscrapers

Fireworks burst over the city

A helicopter flies over the city

A rain cloud passes over the city

Lightning flashes over Seattle

A shooting star shoots

A hot-air balloon drifts over the city

The Space Needle is illuminated with Christmas decorations

A bunch of balloons flies up from behind the buildings

A crescent moon rises

An airship flies over the city

A full moon rises

A plane flies over the city towing a KACL Radio banner

A crane lifts a load over the skyline

A monorail train passes in front of the skyscrapers

A rainbow appears over the city

Nothing happens

> **I was the kid next door's imaginary friend.**
> Emo Philips

JO BRAND — THE INSIDER'S VIEW

Jo Brand is somewhat unusual among comedians in that her experience of mental instability has been strictly from the professional side of the fence. Prior to 1987, when she gave up her job to concentrate full-time on comedy, Brand worked as a psychiatric nurse at the Maudsley Hospital in South London (part of the institution formerly known as "Bedlam").

"I have never been frightened or thought they were odd," Brand has said of people with mental-health problems. "I just thought they were normal human beings who were having a bit of a hard time." In 2003, she and Helen Griffin, a friend from her nursing days, wrote and performed a play entitled *Mental* at the Edinburgh Fringe Festival, based on their experiences at work.

Generally regarded as painfully sane, Brand has increasingly swapped stand-up comedy for family life—she has two small children—but continues to appear frequently on British TV. She is a regular guest on the serious political discussion program *Question Time*, and was recently game enough to take part in the cult makeover show *What Not to Wear* despite, by her own admission, being nobody's idea of a clothes horse.

> **I told my psychiatrist that everyone hates me. He said I was being ridiculous— everyone hasn't met me yet.**
> Grammy Award-winning comedian Rodney Dangerfield

1957

At the age of three, contracted Bell's palsy, a condition that causes a paralysis of the face that can be permanent.

1968

Hit by a car, having deliberately walked into traffic. Spent several days in a coma. Barr was subsequently admitted to a state mental hospital for almost a year, where she was diagnosed with a personality disorder and treated with Thorazine.

Mid-1970s

Spent a period working as a hooker.

1990

Generated a hurricane of controversy with an "unorthodox" rendition of *The Star Spangled Banner* at a baseball game in San Diego. Screeching rather than singing it, she spat like a player and grabbed at her crotch throughout.

1991

Claimed in an interview in *People* magazine that she was physically and sexually assaulted by both her parents as a child. They vehemently denied this and both passed lie-detector tests.

1994

Announced that she had been diagnosed in the past as suffering from depression, obsessive compulsive disorder, agoraphobia and multiple personality disorder (with somewhere between 16 and 21 separate "characters").

1994

Filed for divorce from Tom Arnold claiming domestic violence.

1998

Filed for divorce from her third husband, Ben Thomas, claiming he had threatened to kidnap their son. The couple temporarily patched things up but divorced in 2002.

Excess all areas

WHY ABUSE THE AUDIENCE
WHEN YOU CAN ABUSE YOURSELF?

There's excess and then there was John Belushi. Fans of *The Blues Brothers*, in which the rotund Albanian-American comic and his partner Dan Aykroyd leave a spectacular trail of havoc around Chicago, may not be aware that his character in the film was considerably more restrained than the real thing.

A note in Belushi's medical file gives us an insight into his appetites: "Smokes: three packs a day. Alcohol: drinks socially. Medication: Valium occasionally. Marijuana: smokes four to five times per week. Cocaine: snorts daily, main habit. Mescaline: regularly. Acid: 10 to 20 trips. No heroin. Amphetamines: four kinds. Barbiturates: habit." The doctor adds that, as an afterthought, Belushi confessed to an addiction to Quaaludes as he was leaving the surgery.

Belushi's favorite party game was "cocaine chicken." This involved him cutting an ounce of the drug (that's 28 g) into one giant line several yards long. He would then challenge someone to snort their way to the middle of the line faster than him. It never happened.

The star's unpredictable behavior and less-than-healthy lifestyle also took a toll on Lorne Michaels, his producer on *Saturday Night Live*. On more than one occasion, Belushi burned Michaels's house down, usually by falling asleep while smoking. Matters came to a head one day in 1979 when the inevitable happened: Keith Richards came to town. On hearing that his only serious rival for self-abuse on the planet was in New York at the same time as him, Belushi naturally hooked up with him. One imagines that they had quite a feisty party.

The next day, Belushi somehow staggered into the NBC studio in the Rockefeller Center. He was immediately seen by the company doctor, who then went to see Lorne Michaels. The doctor informed the producer that, in his professional opinion, if Belushi went through with the scheduled filming, there was a 50-50 chance that he would die. "I can live with those odds," growled Michaels.

Not surprisingly, Belushi died in his early 30s . . .

COMEDIANS AND THE BOTTLE

The following have all admitted to serious problems with alcohol, although many are now on the wagon:

Caroline Aherne (aka Mrs. Merton)
Jim Davidson
Jack Dee
W. C. Fields
Charles Hawtrey (*Carry On* actor)
Richard Lewis (American comic/actor)
Dorothy Parker
Richard Pryor
Frank Skinner
Johnny Vegas

HOW TO GROSS OUT YOUR FELLOW PASSENGERS

The author of this book was once on a transatlantic flight and fell into conversation with the woman in the adjoining seat. They began discussing people they had sat next to on previous flights. "I have an amazing story about that," she told him. "The other day, I found myself sitting next to Barry Humphries [the great Australian comedian whose alter-egos include Dame Edna Everage and Sir Les Patterson]. When the cabin staff served up the in-flight meal, he didn't eat his. Instead, he started cutting it up into tiny pieces. Then he mixed everything together—meat, vegetables, dessert, salad, cheese, crackers, the lot—and emptied it into his air-sickness bag. I thought: 'OK, he's slightly mad but he's harmless,' and eventually forgot about it.

"A few hours later, Humphries tapped me on the shoulder and politely asked if I could let him into the aisle because he needed to use the bathroom. I noticed he was clutching the air-sickness bag. He proceeded to walk down the aisle, nonchalant as you like, scooping great handfuls of the congealed contents into his mouth. Within seconds, a stampede of green-looking passengers hurtled toward the bathrooms . . ."

He liked a drink, did W. C. "I drink therefore I am" Fields. Even when he was in a drying-out clinic in Pasadena, California, Fields got through two bottles of gin a day (they were smuggled in by a thoughtful friend). Once, a sympathetic waiter, seeing him evidently suffering from an acute hangover, offered the comedian some seltzer. Fields declined. "I couldn't bear the noise," he declared in agony.

Fields was way too thirsty to abandon the habit when he was working. During filming, he always kept a thermos to hand, filled with what he euphemistically described as "pineapple juice." One day, he got back to his chair to find that someone had tampered with it. "Somebody," he screamed, "has put pineapple juice in my pineapple juice!" In a similar vein, he was once heard to complain: "What contemptible scoundrel has stolen the cork to my lunch?"

Fields liked the bottle, but disliked children with equal intensity. At one stage he launched a hilarious smear campaign against the three-year-old child star Baby Le Roy, with whom he had appeared in a number films. One day, he spiked the toddler's orange juice with gin on set. When Le Roy was unable to stand up, never mind perform for the camera, the comedian called for him to be sacked. "He's no trooper!" Fields called out triumphantly.

> **If I had been around when Rubens was painting, I would have been revered as a fabulous model. Kate Moss? Well, she would have been the paintbrush . . .**
>
> Dawn French

"Awight?" was the catchphrase that brought skinny South London comedian Michael Barrymore to fame, but if you had asked the former Saturday night TV compere—with hits such as *Strike It Lucky* under his belt—the same question in recent years, the only honest answer would have been: "No."

The former Butlins Redcoat's troubles began in 1995 when the British tabloids outed him as a homosexual. This followed an incident in which a drag queen had dragged him onto the stage of one of the capital's better-known gay clubs, having seen through his cunning disguise of a baseball cap.

In 2000, alarm bells started to ring when Barrymore turned sweet-and-lovely presenter Mary Nightingale upside down at an awards ceremony, exposing her underwear and generally overstepping the mark. The following year, he was cautioned for a drugs offense in the aftermath of an episode in which a prostitute claimed that she had been raped in a hotel room paid for by the star.

Shortly afterward, a man was found dead in Barrymore's swimming pool, following a party during which a post-mortem revealed the victim to have ingested copious quantities of alcohol and drugs. When the police arrived, they found that the host had left to check himself into a psychiatric clinic. Barrymore was subsequently arrested on drug charges. Although cleared of any direct responsibility for the death, he has found it difficult to resuscitate his career.

> **Why is there so much controversy about drug testing? I know plenty of guys who would be willing to test any drug they could come up with.**
>
> George Carlin

HEAVYWEIGHTS

The following comedians would all be unlikely to shoot up into the air if you sat opposite them on a seesaw:

John Goodman – said to have weighed more than
350 lbs at his peak

John Candy – 300 lbs

Oliver Hardy – about 300 lbs

Fatty Arbuckle – 300 lbs

Chris Farley – 290 lbs when he died

Bernard Manning – 280 lbs

Jo Brand – newspapers have estimated her weight
at 196 lbs

Robbie Coltrane – God only knows

THAT'S JUST SICK . . .

In 2003, readers of *Maxim* magazine voted the Mr. Creosote scene from Monty Python's 1983 film *The Meaning of Life* the funniest movie moment of all time. It's certainly one of the grossest. Put it this way: Quentin Tarantino found it unbearably disgusting. That's *Quentin Tarantino*, mind you.

The action begins with the heaviest man in the world (Terry Jones in a grotesque bodysuit) waddling into an expensive restaurant. He is seated by the obsequious maitre d' (John Cleese), and immediately calls for a bucket. Then he throws up in it. He proceeds to order the entire menu, plus six crates of brown ale, six bottles of Château La Tour, and a double jeroboam of Champagne. By the end of his meal, Creosote has expanded alarmingly and looks distinctly green about the gills. But Cleese tempts him to a final morsel, a "*wafer*-thin mint." It is one mouthful too many. There's a tearing sound, then the stomach of the fattest man on Earth explodes and the restaurant and its clientele are drenched in semidigested food and bits of gut. Bon appetite.

> **Cocaine is God's way of saying you're making too much money.**
>
> Robin Williams

THE ORIGINAL PET SHOP BOY

When it comes to the greatest headlines in history, "Freddie Starr Ate My Hamster," as *The Sun* proclaimed in 1986, must be a contender. The facts that the Scouse comedian hadn't actually eaten any cuddly rodents, and that the episode turned out to be a PR stunt, were almost beside the point. The important thing was that the British were quite willing to believe the story. After being exposed to Freddie on their televisions for several years, they wouldn't have put it past him.

Born Frederick Fowell, Starr had a tough but colorful upbringing that partly explains his idiosyncratic behavior in later life. At the age of six, he lost the power of speech for two years and was sent away from home to be treated (his doctors diagnosed the condition as psychosomatic). Later he hung out with gangsters and, as a singer, was involved in the buzzing Liverpool and Hamburg music scenes during the 1960s. But Starr's real claim to fame was imitating Adolf Hitler. In Wellington boots. Maybe there was a small part of every Englishman that yearned to yell "Sieg Heil!" and perform an ultramanic goose-step, but now they don't have to—Freddie Starr did it for them.

A serious alcoholic until he quit in 1978, Starr had better luck with the horses—in 1994 his nag Minnehoma won the Grand National. But his animal antics hit the headlines again three years later when he was reported to the RSPCA for throwing live chickens at the audience in a Great Yarmouth gig.

PRISON IMPROVEMENT

When Tim Allen, the star of the hit sitcom *Home Improvement*, first tried stand-up comedy, he instantly realized that he had found his vocation. Unfortunately, he happened to be on bail at the time, having been caught selling cocaine to fellow students at his college in 1978. He subsequently spent two years in a Northern Minnesota jail, an experience which gave him both time and good reason to practice the skills he would need in his chosen career.

Allen had already learned a bit about deflecting bullying with humor as a schoolboy, fate having bestowed on him the unfortunate family name Dick. Now that he was faced with a scarier crowd, his ability to make people laugh proved a life-saver. "Humor is the only way to disarm people who are angry," Allen would later recall. "There was this guy who always wanted to hurt me, but if I did Elmer Fudd I'd get him laughing."

Allen's favorite moment during his incarceration occurred on a bus trip to a neighboring prison, when he somehow managed to slip his handcuffs. He decided he fancied a smoke, so he leaned over the seat in front of him and took a cigarette from the shirt pocket of the fearsome but helpless bank robber seated there. Simultaneously, Allen tapped him on the shoulder with his other hand and asked him for a light. The old lag's face was a picture.

ROCK 'N' ROLLING IN THE AISLES

"Brace yourselves. I'm not kidding. Sam Kinison."
David Letterman, introducing Kinison's first TV performance

A former Pentecostal preacher who sported flowing locks, a bandana and a voice like a cowboy Alsatian riding into the thick of some deafening shootout, Sam Kinison was not a man familiar with the concept of boundaries. Particularly the boundary known as "empty." Once, when holding a raging party at a hotel, cowboy Kinison was distressed to find that his mini bar had run dry, and that the main hotel bar had been locked up for the night. Refusing to let this hinder the event, he resourcefully ordered a fleet of limousines to the hotel, opened them up and directed his guests to the contents of their mini bars. They weren't there to transport anyone; all Kinison was after was the booze.

BILL MURRAY'S MISSPENT YOUTH

As a first-year student at Regis College in Denver, Bill Murray was caught attempting to smuggle an impressive 9 lbs (4 kg) of marijuana through Chicago's O'Hare Airport. The future star of *Saturday Night Live*, *Ghostbusters* and *Lost in Translation* was promptly suspended, allowing him to concentrate on his comedy career.

Murray has an unpredictable streak that has led his friend Dan Aykroyd to describe him as "The Murricaine." He has been known to physically attack hecklers, and once "accidentally" broke Robert de Niro's nose during the filming of *Mad Dog and Glory*.

The extremity of some of Murray's antics may have something to do with the fact that his father was notoriously difficult to make laugh. In fact, the only time Murray recalls succeeding as a child was when he fell off the dining room table while doing a Jimmy Cagney impression and banged his head on one of the metal legs.

STONER COMEDIANS

These comedians have all confessed to a weakness for the weed:

Dan Aykroyd
Jennifer Aniston
Milton Berle
Cheech Marin
Thomas Chong
Ali G
Rodney Dangerfield
Woody Harrelson
Larry Hagman
. . . and that great comedian Bill Clinton
(although, of course, he didn't inhale)

> **I'm not really a heavy smoker anymore. I only get through two lighters a day now.**
>
> Bill Hicks

CRACKING UP

No one could say that Richard Pryor had the easiest start in life. His father was a pimp and his mother a prostitute who worked in a brothel run by his grandmother in Peoria, Illinois. He has told how he was raped by a neighbor at the age of six, abused by the Catholic priest who taught him his catechism and subjected to the sight of his mother "servicing" the local mayor. It was no great surprise, therefore, when the adolescent Pryor started to go off the rails, particularly once he was expelled from school at 14 for punching a teacher in the face.

Pryor's saving grace has been his talent for seeing the funny side of adversity. In his case this has been considerable, encompassing seven divorces, two heart attacks, quadruple heart bypass surgery and a diagnosis of multiple sclerosis in 1986. But Pryor is possibly at his funniest when recounting tales of his drug and alcohol fueled past. The ultimate example occurred in 1980, when he managed to set fire to himself while smoking a crack pipe. Once ablaze, the comedian jumped out of his apartment window and ran down the street screaming. The incident, one of the first to bring the dangerous cocaine derivative to public attention, came very close to killing him. More than 50% of his skin was burned away and Pryor was in intensive care for six weeks.

> **I love blackjack.**
> **I'm not addicted to gambling. I'm addicted to sitting in a semicircle.**
>
> Late US comedian Mitch Hedberg

Family
affairs

SEX, MARRIAGE, AND THE BATTLE
OF THE GENDERS

CHAPLIN'S DOWNFALL

In 1943, a pregnant 22-year-old actress named Joan Barry burst into the office of LA gossip columnist Hedda Hopper and gave her what she had long been looking for: some dirt on Charlie Chaplin. Barry, who had met Chaplin two years earlier, claimed that he was the father of her unborn child.

After the meeting, Hopper wrote an article that spelled the end of Chaplin's Hollywood career. He was arrested on charges of "white slavery" (taking a woman across state lines for "immoral purposes") under the 1910 Mann Act, a piece of legislation that in practice allowed the police to prosecute almost any actively heterosexual male they fancied.

Chaplin's big mistake, apart from a weakness for young women (he twice married 16-year-olds), had been arousing the suspicions of the FBI. Somewhat naively, he had taken part in fundraising activities on behalf of the USSR, America's supposed wartime ally. Thus no sooner had his first trial been abandoned than he faced a trumped-up paternity charge. Although Chaplin admitted that he had slept with Barry, medical evidence proved that he could not be her child's father, but this was deemed inadmissible. The court also overlooked the fact that Barry was demonstrably unstable, having, for example, burst into Chaplin's apartment with a gun on one occasion when he tried to end the relationship. He was ordered to pay child maintenance.

SIX MEGA-CAMP COMEDIANS

Kenneth Williams

Frankie Howerd

Larry Grayson

John Inman

Julian Clary

Graham Norton

SEX SCANDALS INVOLVING COMEDIANS

Eddie Murphy

In 1997, Murphy was stopped on Santa Monica Boulevard with a 20-year-old Samoan transvestite prostitute named Atisone Seiuli in his passenger seat. Seiuli was promptly arrested, but no charges were brought against the comedian.

Bill Cosby

In February 2005, an unnamed Canadian woman alleged that the comedian had drugged her prior to a sex session the previous year. Police said that Cosby would not face charges.

Hugh Grant

The *Four Weddings* and *Notting Hill* star's moment of indiscretion with LA hooker Divine Brown was one of the top tabloid stories of the 1990s.

Angus Deayton

The former presenter of the satirical BBC quiz show *Have I Got News for You* found his position untenable after a Sunday newspaper ran a story about him taking cocaine in a hotel room with a prostitute.

Oscar Wilde

Wound up in Reading Prison after a dalliance with "Bosey."

> ## The quickest way to a man's heart is through his rib cage.
> Jo Brand, or "The Sea Monster," as she initially styled herself

COMEDIANS WITH MULTIPLE SPOUSES

Richard Pryor 7 wives, 8 marriages (married one twice)

Stan Laurel 4 wives, 5 marriages (married one twice)

Jim Davidson 4 wives

Charlie Chaplin 4 wives

Peter Sellers 4 wives

John Cleese 3 wives

GROUCHO THE LUCKY GARDENER

Always one for the ladies, Groucho Marx had a ready line in risqué jokes. When the rabbi conducting his first wedding announced that the couple were there to be joined in holy matrimony, he quipped: "It may be holy to you, but we have other ideas!" On another occasion he found himself in a lift in Venice with a group of priests. When one of them confessed that his mother was a great fan, Marx replied: "I didn't know you guys were allowed to have mothers."

In a similarly naughty vein, when *Playboy* magazine asked him what he would do differently if he had his life over again, Groucho answered: "Try more positions."

Once, Groucho was working in the garden of his California house when a rich, middle-aged woman drove by in a Cadillac. As she currently had a domestic vacancy, she wound down her window and summoned him over imperiously. "Gardener," she inquired, "how much does the lady of the house pay you?" Quick as a flash, Marx replied: "Oh, I don't get paid in dollars. The lady of the house just lets me sleep with her."

PEE WEE'S UNFORTUNATE ADVENTURE

The diminutive star of *Pee Wee's Big Adventure* (1985), played by actor Paul Ruebens, was a naiive child-man with a bow tie and trousers several times too small for him. There were therefore a lot of "I told you sos" when Ruebens was arrested on public indecency charges in 1991, having been caught pleasuring himself in an adult cinema in Sarasota, Florida. Although Ruebens publicly denied the charges—in 2004, he said: "I maintained at the time I was innocent and I maintain that still"—he negotiated a deal with Sarasota County Court whereby he paid a fine and avoided a trial. The incident was effectively the end of the Pee Wee character.

Ruebens has gone on to play small parts in *Buffy the Vampire Slayer*, *Batman Returns* and *The Nightmare Before Christmas*, but his career has never fully recovered. In 2002, his PR problem was compounded when he was arrested again, this time for possession of child pornography. The comedian countered that he was merely an avid collector of "vintage erotica" and was the victim of a witch hunt. The charge against him was eventually dropped when he pleaded guilty to the lesser offence of public obscenity.

NINE LESBIAN (OR BI-) COMEDIANS

Ellen DeGeneres ● Sandra Bernhard

Kate Clinton ● Sandy Toksvig

Lily Tomlin ● Margaret Cho

Elvira Kurt ● Rosie O'Donnell

Suzanne Westenhoefer

> **I wasn't kissing her. I was whispering in her mouth.**
> Chico Marx, after his wife had caught him kissing a chorus girl

WAYANS WORLD

US showbiz dynasty the Wayans family has unleashed some of the most memorable film parodies of the last 20 years. Its creative nucleus is Keenan Ivory, the co-writer of Robert Townsend's 1987 satire on black movie stereotypes, *Hollywood Shuffle*, and star and director of the action-movie/cop-comedy, *I'm Gonna Git You Sucka* (1988), which features possibly the most painful bunion scene ever committed to film. From there, he marshaled the talents of his sister Kim and brothers Damon, Marlon, and Shawn into the popular US sketch show *In Living Color* (1990–1994), which not only broke the family talent, but also gave exposure to a future comic master by the name of Jim Carrey.

The satirical streak continued unabated with the 1994 film, *A Low Down Dirty Shame*, and arguably hit its peak—certainly in as far as its title— with the lampoon of the mid 1990s "conscience" films about young black men involved in gang violence, *Don't Be a Menace to South Central While Drinking Your Juice in the Hood* (1996). By then, Damon had already gone into more mainstream action-comedy by teaming up with Bruce Willis in 1991's *The Last Boy Scout.*

Keenan himself would gain similar credentials, pairing with Steven Seagal on *The Glimmer Man* (1996). The troupe later developed the Scary Movie franchise and the trans-racial undercover cop farce, *White Chicks* (2004). With their dedication to comedy as a way of life and an ironclad family work ethic, the Wayanses have shown over the years that, sometimes, nepotism isn't such a bad thing.

THE ROYLE FAMILY

Arguably Britain's favorite fictional family, the Royles never do anything except sit in front of the TV smoking and chatting. This might seem an unpromising formula for a sitcom ("where's the drama in that?" the uninitiated might ask) but *The Royle Family* has one great strength: its audience can't help but identify with the protagonists. It consists, by definition, of a load of Brits watching telly. Dad Jim (Ricky Tomlinson) is fat, lazy, unemployed and opinionated, and rarely gets up except when he needs an "Eartha" (as in "Kitt"). Mum Barbara (Sue Johnston) runs around trying to keep a semblance of order and occasionally remembers to reprimand the others for swearing. Their daughter Denise (Caroline Aherne) is fantastically inactive, except for permanently fiddling with her nails and sometimes asking her mother to scold her younger brother Antony (Ralf Little) because she can't be bothered. Then there's her taciturn boyfriend Dave (Craig Cash), the odd neighbor who pops in and that's about it.

Part of the genius of the show's casting lies in the fact that Johnston and Tomlinson played another well-known TV couple for many years. Only Sheila and Bobby Grant were miserable in *Brookside*, whereas Jim and Barbara are rather jolly.

Ah, yes, divorce, from the Latin word meaning "to
rip out a man's genitals through his wallet."
Robin Williams

BENNY HILL

Once described as a saucy seaside postcard brought to life, Benny Hill grew rich playing out the fantasies of repressed Anglo-Saxon males while simultaneously ridiculing them. A typical Hill sketch featured him chasing a bunch of scantily clad, large-breasted girls around on speeded up film. Occasionally, he managed to pinch one of the bottoms of the so-called "Hill's Angels." Not the most sophisticated stuff, but it earned the former milkman from Southampton millions. Hill got his television breakthrough in 1969 with *The Benny Hill Show*. Ten years later, the show was sold to America, where it became (and remains) an enormous hit. But Hill inevitably fell foul of the political correctness movement, and his program was axed in 1989.

Despite his lecherous TV persona, Hill kept his private life extremely private. He never married, having twice proposed and twice been turned down, and never owned a house or car despite his fortune. He died in 1992.

WOODY AND SOON-YI

When, in 2001, Woody Allen announced that he had finally stopped seeing his psychoanalyst, late-night talk-show host, Jay Leno quipped that: "If, after 40 years, you've married your own daughter, then I guess you can figure it isn't working!" To be fair to Allen, Soon-Yi Previn, who Allen married in Venice in 1997, was not in fact remotely his daughter. She was, rather, the adopted daughter of his former partner, Mia Farrow. But this didn't prevent the inevitable barrage of mother-in-law jokes.

Allen's affair with his common-law stepdaughter first came to light in 1992, when Farrow was less than pleased to find pornographic photos of her on the comedian's mantelpiece. The furious actress, who allegedly broke a chair over Soon-Yi's head, subsequently accused Allen of having abused their jointly adopted 17-year-old daughter, Dylan. He was cleared of all charges, but has looked paler and more uncomfortable ever since. Bizarrely, the Soon-Yi scandal coincided almost exactly with the release of *Husbands and Wives*, in which Allen and Farrow play a couple whose marriage hits the rocks when he starts dating a 20-year-old student.

CROSS-DRESSING COMEDIANS

Eddie Izzard
also does it in his spare time

Hinge and Bracket
preposterous "posh lady" duo of the 1970s

Flip Wilson
NBC host had alter ego called Geraldine

Milton Berle
"Mr. Television" liked to totter about stage in high heels

Dick Emery
"Oh, you are awful—but I like you!"

Kenny Everett
"Of course, it's all done in the best paaaaasible taste!"

Les Dawson and Roy Barraclough
Cissy and Ada

Paul O'Grady
Lilly Savage

David Walliams and Matt Lucas
Emily and Florence: "We are ladies you know!"

> I was cleaning out the attic the other day with the wife. Filthy, dirty, and covered in cobwebs. But she's good with the kids.
>
> Tommy Cooper

DAME EDNA EVERAGE

In 1955, Australian comedian Barry Humphries gave birth to a monster. Dame Edna Everage began life as a humble Melbourne housewife, but has risen to become (according to her website) ". . . [an] investigative journalist, social anthropologist, talk-show host, swami, children's book illustrator, spin-doctor, megastar and icon." Blessed with natural wisteria hair from birth, her rise to fame was, with hindsight, a foregone conclusion.

Although she has been a widow for more than a decade, Dame Edna remains acutely aware of her feminine charms. "You know, in Australia I'm a sex symbol like Claudia Schiffer is here," she reminded the Germans on a recent visit to their country. She boasts that her doctor has declared her "perfectly healthy and still able to have grandchildren."

Everage also has a reputation for sexual frankness. "I know body hair bothers some women, but a lot of men like a fluffy partner," she once observed. And she has a sharp answer for anyone who dares to question her identity: "People think Barry Humphries and I are the same person. Well, let them talk to my gynaecologist!" she threatens.

THE DEATH OF CHIVALRY

Billy Crystal is famously monogamous. His wife Janice was his first and only date. But his assistant Lacy thought she was in luck when the pair found themselves in Chicago one night when every room in the city seemed to have been booked for a sales convention.

Eventually they found a room with twin beds and decided to share it. During the night, Lacy invoked a time-honored female ploy and announced that she was cold. "Well, Lacy," Crystal responded, "How would you like to be Mrs. Crystal for the night?" "I'd love to be Mrs Crystal for the night," she replied. "Then get up and shut the window then!" the comedian barked.

Mock thy neighbor

COMEDY ON A GLOBAL SCALE

MIND YOUR LANGUAGE

Now regarded as about the least politically correct sitcom in the history of the world, *Mind Your Language* was set in a London language school of the 1970s. In essence, the program was an excuse for the writers to have fun with national stereotypes. In the show's defense, at least it gave 10-year-olds somewhere to start when trying to make sense of an increasingly multicultural society. Provided, that is, that no one took it too seriously. Here are some of the key characters:

Jeremy Brown (Barry Evans)
awkward English teacher

Giovanni Capello (George Camiller)
lustful, gesticulating Italian

Juan Cervantes (Ricardo Montez)
lustful, macho Spaniard

Maximillian Papandrious (Kevork Malikyan)
lustful Greek

Danielle Favre (Francoise Pascal)
sexy, flirtatious French woman

Anna Schmidt (Jacki Harding)
housewife with coiled pigtails

Chung Su-Lee (Pik-Sen Lim)
Rampantly Maoist Chinese student

Ali Nadim (Dino Shafeek)
Pakistani given to waving his head from side to side

Ranjeet Singh (Albert Moses)
the class Sikh

Ingrid Svenson (Anna Bergman)
Sexually liberated Swedish blonde

During the communist era, few Russians dared to openly criticize their government. Instead, they expressed their views through bone-dry *anekdoty* (jokes). A favorite device was the Armenian Radio joke, so called because Armenians were popularly perceived as clever and subversive. It always began with the formula: "This is Armenian Radio. Our listeners asked us X, Y or Z." Here are some choice examples:

This is Armenian Radio. Our listeners asked us . . .

What should we do if the western borders of the USSR are opened?
We're answering: "Rush to Siberia to avoid being crushed in the stampede."

Why is our government not in a hurry to land our men on the moon?
We're answering: "What if they refuse to come back?"

What starts with an "R" but never ends?
We're answering: "Reorganization." (Which would actually begin with a Р in Russian script, but never mind.)

Why did Lenin have regular shoes but Stalin wore boots?
We're answering: "In Lenin's time, Russia was only ankle-deep in sh*t."

Is there life on other planets?
We're answering: "There is also no life on other planets."

> **There was an Englishman and an Irishman and a Pakistani sitting in a bar . . . fine example of an integrated multicultural community!**
>
> PC comedian Bernard Righton in *The Fast Show*

I find it hard to say, because when I was there it seemed to be shut.

Clement Freud (radio wit, journalist, and grandson of Sigmund Freud) when asked for his impressions of New Zealand. Freud sounds a bit like the cartoon hound Droopy.

ALI G

Sacha Baron Cohen has made a career out of playing on contemporary society's awkwardness regarding race and ethnicity. His most famous creation, Ali G, is an Asian man played by a Jewish man pretending to be a black man. Cohen uses Ali to ruthlessly exploit celebrities' terror of being perceived as racist, patronizing or out of touch with "da Yout(h)."

Among Ali's most memorable questions to date are:

"Why do they call it the welfare state? Is it coz it's well fair?"
to veteran socialist politician Tony Benn

"When can you murder someone?"
to controversial judge James Pickles

"When is man going to walk on da sun?"
to astronaut Buzz Aldrin

"Jesus. Does he really have a beard?"
to the Bishop of Corsham

If any of his interviewees has the temerity to fight back, Ali has a potent weapon in his locker. "Is it because I is black?" he asks. Nobody has yet dared to point out that he isn't.

In 2002, ahead of a soccer game between England and Albania in Tirana, an Englishman ran onto the field dribbling a football and the home crowd exploded with delight. Who was this man with such power to move Albanians? David Beckham, you might assume. Wrong. It was 87-year-old knockabout comedian Norman Wisdom. When he was halfway across the field, Pitkini, as Wisdom is known to the locals, tripped himself up on purpose. It was a trick he had performed in countless black-and-white movies, and it brought the house down.

The key to Wisdom's almost godlike celebrity in Albania was the country's former dictator Enver Hoxha. Although a man who might, for instance, dismiss a minister by shooting him in the head, Hoxha was drawn to Wisdom's brand of comedy. He liked that there was no swearing, politics, or violence: such innocuous stuff would make good fodder for his subjects. He also managed to convince himself that Pitkini's troubled relationship with his boss Mr. Grimshaw symbolized the proletariat's struggle with the bourgeoisie. As a result, Norman Wisdom films were about the only things shown on Albania's few televisions for decades.

Wisdom reciprocates the adoration by involving himself in Albanian charitable projects. When he announced his intention to retire from comedy on his 90th birthday in 2005, the country went into mourning.

Americans have different ways of saying things. They say "elevator," we say "lift" . . . they say "president," we say "stupid psychopathic git."
Alexei Sayle

> **New Zealand is a country of thirty thousand million sheep, three million of whom think they're human.**
>
> Barry Humphries

GERMAN HUMOR

The rest of the world sometimes wonders whether such a thing exists. The British website www.anenglishmanscastle.com recently proposed the following as a typical example of German comedy:

> "Knock knock."
> "Who's there?"
> "Tom."
> "Tom who?"
> "Tom Buchanan."
> "Pleased to meet you, Tom!"

This may be a trifle unkind, but there is statistical evidence to suggest that Germans en masse are not the funniest people on Earth (although they do have a marked taste for slapstick—*Mr. Bean* is a big hit in Germany). They do have a sense of humor, but its use is restricted to certain times and places, and from the perspective of less analytical nationalities it can lack spontaneity.

In 1999, a study at the University of Berkeley in California found that whereas the French and Italians typically laugh for 18 minutes daily and the British for 15, the average German spends a mere six minutes of the day indulging in laughter. When the news broke, a horrified group of Teutonic comedians formed the German Laughter Club in an attempt to bring the national average up to 20 minutes. Only a native could fathom whether they were being literal or self-deprecatingly funny (or indeed whether the distinction even applies in Germany).

> **Boy, those French, they have a different word for everything!**
>
> Steve Martin

THE BULGARIAN MUSEUM OF COMEDY

On April 1, 1972 (we kid you not), the state-sanctioned House of Humor and Satire opened for business in the Bulgarian town of Gabrovo. The museum, which bears the legend: "Welcome and Good Riddance" over its entrance, has four floors and 10 exhibition halls. Every May, it is the center of an international comedy festival held in the town.

Some of the exhibits are more geared to the idiosyncrasies of the Bulgarian sense of humor. The First Private Anecdote Bank, which credits customers who take out a loan with one joke, may be lost on many outsiders, but everyone can appreciate the Hall of Distorting Mirrors. There are also masks, cartoons, paintings, amusing sculptures and a humor research department.

The House of Humor and Satire also sells a range of merchandise, much of it featuring a stylized cat and/or the Gabrovo town slogan: "The world survives because it laughs."

> **Canadians are just Mexicans with sweaters.**
>
> US comedian Dave Fulton

Race is a tricky subject for comedians, particularly in America, where racial tensions are seldom far from the surface. But precisely because it is a semi-taboo topic, it can prove a rich vein of humor for those skilful enough to mine it. With comedy, you can sometimes say the unsayable, as Richard Pryor and Chevy Chase proved in a classic *Saturday Night Live* sketch.

The genius of the sketch is its setting in a context in which neither man is ostensibly responsible for what he is saying. Pryor plays an unemployed black man being interviewed for a job by Chase. To get the ball rolling, Chase suggests a game of word association. This starts off innocently enough, with exchanges on the lines of "Tree" from Chase followed by the response "Dog" from Pryor. As the pace accelerates, however, the two men begin to reveal their true colors, and in more ways than one:

Chase:	Pryor:
"White?"	"Black"
"Negro?"	"Whitey"
"Colored?"	"Redneck"
"Tar baby?"	"Peckerwood"
"Spear-chucker?"	"White trash"
"Jungle bunny?"	"Honkey"
"Nigger?"	"DEAD Honkey"

**There'll always be an England,
even if it's in Hollywood.**

Bob Hope

WHO TELLS JOKES ABOUT WHO?

The English joke about...The Irish

The Irish...People from County Kerry

The Welsh...The English

Spaniards...Gallegos (folk from Galica)
and Argentinians (often of Gallego descent)

Everyone else in South America..Argentinians

Argentinians...Bolivians

Egyptians (Semitic)...Nubians

The French...Belgians

Israelis...Kurdish Jews

South Africans (of British Descent)..Afrikaners

Iranians...Azerbaijanis

Canadians...Newfoundlanders

Americans...Poles and Mexicans

Jewish people...Other Jewish people

Well, most of our electric companies are owned by
the Americans. The prime minister is owned by the
Ulster Unionists. Hong Kong is going back to China.
The only thing we actually own is Northern Ireland,
and we nicked that!
The Mark Thomas Comedy Product,
on the state of the UK in 1995

> I read in the newspapers they are going to
> have 30 minutes of intellectual stuff on
> television every Monday from 7:30 to 8:00
> to educate America. They couldn't educate
> America if they started at 6:30.
>
> Groucho Marx

STAVROS

Stavros was a Greek kebab shop owner with a vivid but mangled way with the English language. He first hit British TV screens in the mid-to-late 1980s in the locale of *Saturday Night Live*, and went on to star in his creator's series *The Harry Enfield Show*. Many of his catchphrases became household expressions, from "innit?" (a variant of "know what I mean?" which Stavros didn't invent but certainly popularized) to "Up the Arse!" (he was a passionate Arsenal supporter), to his description of Margaret Thatcher as "The Ironing Lady."

From the moment Stavros first greeted viewers with a cheery: "Hello, peeps!," there was a palpable sense that here was something new. This was not so much a comedian playing a character as a character dropping in of his own accord. (It helped that Enfield was not yet famous in his own right.) With hindsight, Stavros was perhaps not quite as new as people first thought—we'd seen the likes of Hancock before—but he certainly launched a wave of character-based comedy in the UK that has yet to break.

The friendly Greek character was based on a real kebab shop owner, Adam Athanaffiou, who ran an establishment in the London street in which Enfield shared a flat with fellow comedian Paul Whitehouse.

In 2002, Dr. Richard Wiseman of the University of Hertfordshire announced the result of a year-long quest to find the world's funniest joke. The LaughLab project had encompassed 40,000 jokes and almost two million ratings on a scale of one to five.

Wiseman's research revealed several striking patterns:

The Irish, British, Australians, and New Zealanders preferred jokes relying on word play.

For some reason, jokes with about 103 words were particularly popular. The full version of the most popular of all came in at 102 words.

The French, Belgians, and Danes liked offbeat, surreal humor.
The Germans found everything reasonably funny.

Americans and Canadians tended to like jokes where the central character is made to look stupid, either by themselves or someone else.

Here is the winner. Hold onto your sides . . .

"Two hunters are out in the woods when one of them collapses. He doesn't seem to be breathing and his eyes are glazed. The other guy takes out his phone and calls the emergency services.

"He gasps: 'My friend is dying! What can I do?' The operator says: 'Calm down, I can help. First, let's make sure he's dead . . .' There is a silence, then a gunshot is heard. Back on the phone, the guy says: 'OK, now what?'"

Wiseman noted that this joke, unlike many of its competitors, had a universal appeal. It was awarded high marks by all ages, sexes, and nationalities involved in the survey.

> **The Greeks — dirty and impoverished descendants of a bunch of la-de-da fruit salads who invented democracy and then forgot how to use it while walking around dressed like girls.**
>
> P. J. O'Rourke

ICELANDIC HUMOR

Icelandic humor is so deadpan that the uninitiated often fail to detect its existence. It has been said that when a Scandinavian tells you that the house is on fire, you can tell that they're joking if they say: "The house is on fire!" If, on the other hand, they say: "The house is on fire!" you can be sure that they're deadly serious. Icelanders tend to take this dry approach to an extreme, occasionally tempering it with a surreal streak that reflects the weird natural environment in which they live.

The problem with the straight-faced delivery that characterizes Icelandic jokes is that they tend to lose their effect when written down. Take, for example, this one from Robert Asgeirson:

"You will have truly mastered the Icelandic language when you can sip coffee from a saucer through a sugar lump between your teeth while saying . . ." At this point we have to admit defeat, because whatever needs to be said is: a) incomprehensible to non-Icelanders, b) impossible for them to pronounce, and which c) can only be written on a computer with the aid of special software. Apparently it means "nice to see you" in Icelandic.

Bitterness bites

CONFLICT, CONTROVERSY, AND INSULTS

You could:

. . . imply that they are drunk
"I'm sorry, I don't speak alcoholic."

. . . physically assault them
as Bill Murray did in his youth

. . . encourage the audience to do it for you
like Dave Chapelle ("Punch him in the kidneys!")

. . . use an old chestnut like
"This is what happens when cousins get married."

. . . suggest they are childish, for example, by saying
"I hope your face clears up," or, "It's OK, I remember my first pint, too."

. . . imply that they have a menial job
"Don't tell me how to do my job. Do I go to your job and tell you
how to sweep up?" (Billy Connolly)

. . . insult them sexually
"Good to see you back in men's clothing again," is often effective, as is
"Save your breath—you'll need it later to blow up your girlfriend!"

. . . make them feel self-conscious by asking
"Hello! What have you come as?" (Julian Clary)

. . . get a bouncer to take them outside and have a quiet word with them.
This was Tom Stade's tactic during one gig at London's Comedy Store.

Chris Morris, the bad boy of contemporary British comedy, was once pictured on the front cover of the *Daily Mail* beneath the headline "Britain's Sickest Man." The cause of the furore was an episode of Morris's Channel 4 series *Brass Eye* in which the comedian had lampooned the media's current obsession with paedophilia. Among other outrages, he had persuaded the rock star Phil Collins to walk around in a T-shirt bearing the slogan "Nonce Sense." ("Nonce" is a jail term for "sex offender"). Morris was right about the media hypocrisy—the *Daily Star*, for instance, printed its condemnation of the program opposite a feature about the budding breasts of 15-year-old singer Charlotte Church—but this didn't stop Channel 4 from firing him.

Those familiar with Morris's CV would have known not to take him too seriously. He had begun his career as a "regular" TV news reporter, but kept getting fired for inserting satirical footage of his own into the broadcasts. As a result of his experiences in orthodox television, when Morris moved into comedy, the spoof news items in which he specialized still had an authentic feel. This was the key to their genius, and the reason why so many people fell for them. But as Morris's dismissal demonstrated, Hell hath no fury like public figures made to look stupid.

Morris's greatest achievement in this area was probably the episode of *Brass Eye* devoted to "cake." This was a spurious recreational drug from the Czech Republic which Morris claimed was posing a major threat to Britain's youth. Several celebrities were suckered into campaigning for "cake" to be banned. The artist Rolf Harris was filmed warning would-be users about a dreadful side-effect called "Czech Neck," and the Tory MP David Amess was even moved to ask a question about "cake" in parliament.

> **I never forget a face, but in your case I'll make an exception.**
>
> Groucho Marx

THE LIFE OF BRIAN

Depending on your point of view, *The Life of Brian* (1979) is either a shocking exercise in exploitative blasphemy or Monty Python's finest hour. These observations may help you decide:

In 2004, *Total Film* magazine deemed *The Life of Brian* the fifth-best British film of all time.

The film was banned for a year in Norway.

The Swedes responded by marketing the film as: "So funny that the Norwegians banned it!"

It kicks off with the following exchange, the three wise men having initially picked the wrong address:
Mandy (Brian's mother) "What star sign is he?"
First Wise Man "Capricorn."
Mandy "Capricorn, eh? What are they like then?"
First Wise Man (horrified) "Oh, but he is the son of God, our messiah . . ."
Second Wise Man ". . . King of the Jews!"
Mandy "And that's Capricorn, is it?"

JUVENILE BUT SATISFYING . . .

Wayne's World (1992) focuses on the adventures of two irreverent Illinois teenagers, Wayne (Mike Myers) and his geeky sidekick Garth (Dana Carvey). The boys have their own public access TV show, which is quickly snapped up by a local network. When they arrive at the studio to make their debut on "straight" television, they are determined not to take things too solemnly. Accordingly, while they are interviewing their first guest, a dull video arcade owner named Noah Vanderhoff, Wayne holds up a series of placards to the camera. They read (in order):
"Sphincter Boy,"
"He Blows Goats, I Have Proof," and
"This Man Has No Penis."

WHEN THE BOOT'S ON THE OTHER FOOT

Comedians tend to be good at dishing out insults, but sometimes they have to take a dose of their own medicine . . .

"If people don't sit at Chaplin's feet, he goes out and stands where they are sitting"—Herman Mankievicz on *The Little Tramp*

"When they asked Jack Benny to do something for the Actor's Orphanage, he shot both his parents and moved in"—Bob Hope

"A fellow with the inventiveness of Albert Einstein but the attention span of Daffy Duck"—Tom Shales on Robin Williams

"He emits an air of overwhelming vanity combined with some unspecific nastiness, like a black widow spider in heat. But nobody seems to notice. He could be reciting *Fox's Book of Martyrs* in Finnish and these people would be rolling out of their seats"—Roger Gellert on John Cleese

THE DICEMAN

Andrew "Dice" Clay is a Brooklyn-born comedian with a single mission: to offend as many people as possible. Taking his stage name from the title of a Luke Rhinehart novel about an amoral character who decides what to do by rolling a dice, Clay was at the forefront of the "assault" comedy movement during the 1990s. His act boiled down to a combination of insults directed at women, gays, ethnic minorities and his audiences, and lewd versions of nursery rhymes.

Clay's biggest commercial success was the R-rated album "The Day the Laughter Died" (1990). This was a recording of an unscripted two-hour show in which Clay aimed to clear the auditorium by offending members of the audience to the point that they walked out. He managed a similar trick with the Irish singer Sinead O'Connor on *Saturday Night Live*, though given her impulsive behavior, this may not have been as much of a feat.

In 1995, the Diceman tried to improve his public image by taking on the role of a caring family man in the CBS series *Bless This House*. Clay couldn't stand the experience and the show was quickly pulled.

> ## What do you think of the show so far? (throws voice) "Rubbish!"
> Eric Morecambe

CLOSET FEMINIST?

Roy "Chubby" Brown is a plump, Middlesborough-born comic who performs in a multicolored patchwork jacket and a flying helmet. When he goes on stage, he launches into a routine so blue that he is effectively unbroadcastable. As a result, he relies on word of mouth to attract his audience. It works pretty well: about 350,000 people come to see him perform live every year.

The curious thing about Brown is that his stage persona is seriously at odds with his natural character. The former had to be coaxed out of him by his manager George Forster, who realized that the wave of political correctness that swept through British comedy during the 1980s had left a large hole in the market. "At first he had difficulty swearing," claims Brown's website. It adds: "He is really poking fun at male inadequacy. A third of his audience are women who can relate his act to the men in their lives." Lest anyone think this is just posturing, in 2003, Brown was fined £200 for hitting a member of the public over the head with an umbrella on Blackpool pier. The man's crime? Swearing!

> ## Why are we honoring this man? Have we run out of human beings?
> Milton Berle (at a function for the sports broadcaster Howard Cosell)

> ## Is Elizabeth Taylor fat? Her favorite food is seconds.
>
> Joan Rivers

BERNARD MANNING

Bernard Manning is a completely unreconstructed Mancunian comedian who has somehow become a post-modern media star. The bulky comic, who always has a pint of beer to hand, first hit British television screens in the 1970s show *The Comedians*. His brand of comedy soon became unfashionable, reliant as it was on jokes about immigrants and mothers-in-law, but Manning never saw this as a reason to modify his act. He enjoyed being a dinosaur too much.

For many years Manning was persona non grata on UK TV. Instead, he worked the northern comedy circuit and concentrated on running his own club, The Embassy, in a suburb of Manchester. Then the media suddenly decided that he was perfect for "ironic" documentaries. In 2002, Manning was the surprise presenter of an episode of BBC Radio's *Great Lives* devoted to his idol Mother Theresa. The following year, Channel 4 flew him to India to see how his brand of comedy would go down with the locals. The result was Bernard's *Bombay Dreams*, which included a memorable scene in which his act bombed at the Bombay Gymkhana Club.

Despite his newfound respectability, Manning has never managed to avoid controversy for long. In 2003, a scandal erupted when it emerged that his agent had booked him to entertain delegates at a conference of the ultra right wing BNP (British National Party). Nevertheless, he has forged an unlikely friendship with black activist Darcus Howe. When the pair met, Manning asked Howe where he lived. On hearing that he lived in Brixton, the comedian said: "I went there once. I could be your daddy!" Howe was delighted.

ALF GARNETT

Alf Garnett, the belligerent cockney star of the long-running series *Till Death Us Do Part*, proves the rule that people don't have to like a character to find them watchable. The BBC website describes Garnett as: "an ill-educated, shockingly opinionated, loud-mouthed, appallingly tempered, deeply angry, Tory voting, prudish, monarchist bigot, a deeply working-class man who nonetheless had no time for his kind and wouldn't hear a bad word said about the rich and the privileged."

The series was set in an impoverished suburb of East London, where Garnett lived with his downtrodden wife Elsie (usually addressed as: "You silly moo!"), his trendy daughter Rita and her left-wing republican husband Mike, or "You Scouse git!" as Alf preferred to call him. (Not uninterestingly, Tony Booth, the actor who played Mike, had a daughter called Cherie, also known as Mrs. Tony Blair). Garnett ranted, raved and fought with them all. He also broke new ground by using a range of racial epithets never before heard on British TV.

Although Johnny Speight, the writer of the show, was an Irish communist and its star Warren Mitchell an Australian Jew, *Till Death Us Do Part* was regularly panned in the press for supposedly promoting racism. The *Financial Times* once described the program as: "The rampaging, howling embodiment of all the most vulgar and odious prejudices that slop about in the bilges of the national mind." Speight and Mitchell took this as an occupational hazard: if you try to be satirical, some people are bound to take you seriously.

> **I've just been fisting Norman Lamont.**
> Julian Clary, of the then-British Chancellor of the Exchequer, who had preceded him onstage at the televised 1993 British Comedy Awards

Imagine pitching this idea for a sitcom to a bunch of high-powered television executives: "It's about a bunch of army medics during the Korean War, living in awful conditions in the jungle and dealing with carnage on a daily basis. But there's plenty of scope for laughs. Oh yeah, and we've got a great theme tune, too. It's called 'Suicide is Painless.'" You might, frankly, expect to get short shrift. Yet CBS commissioned just such a series in 1972, and it ran for 11 years. Of course it helped that it was based on the highly successful movie of the same name released two years previously.

M*A*S*H followed the adventures of the 4,077th Mobile Army Surgical Hospital in Korea, but many felt that it was actually a veiled commentary on the Vietnam War (still in progress when the series started). The producers always denied this, saying that M*A*S*H was about war in general, but the dark humor certainly fitted the spirit of the time. It was premised on the idea that in hellish situations, people badly need something to laugh at.

In 1983, almost 106 million Americans assembled in front of their TVs to bid farewell to Hawkeye, Hot Lips and co. "Goodbye, Farewell, and Amen" is the most watched episode of any television series ever, having attracted 77% of the US audience.

> **Shut your festering gob you tit! Your type really makes me puke, you vacuous, toffee-nosed, malodorous pervert!**
>
> *Monty Python* sketch in which a man looking for an argument in a surreal office building goes into the "Abuse" office by mistake

> **God is supposed to have made man in his own image. It would be a great shock to Christians everywhere if God looked like you, Baldrick.**
>
> Edmund Blackadder

THE DANGERS OF DUNDEE

Anyone contemplating a career in stand-up comedy should avoid Dundee, at least until they know what they are doing. This is because the Scottish city is the birthplace of the modern heckler.

"Heckling" was originally a term used in the textile trade for the act of teasing out fibers of flax or hemp. The Dundee of the late-18th and early-19th centuries had a reputation for the radicalism of its workforce, its textile laborers in particular. The town's hecklers were an especially feisty bunch, described by the Rev. George Gilfillan (writing in 1886) as notable "for their knowledge, irregular diligence, occasional bouts of dissipation, great interest in politics and expertness in political conversation." The Dundee hecklers developed a working routine whereby one of them would read out the day's newspapers while the others got on with the heckling. Invariably, the reading would be interrupted by sarcastic interjections in thick Scottish accents.

The poet Robbie Burns worked as a heckler for a time, having become excited by the economic possibilities of flax during the 1780s. He hated it. Celebrity hecklers in the modern sense include Statler and Waldorf, the grumpy old men from *The Muppet Show*.

Old-time comedy

JESTERS, PHILOSOPHERS, AND HOLY FOOLS

The following witticisms are taken from the *Philogelos* ("The Laughter Lover"), a joke book popular in the Greek-speaking world during the fourth and fifth centuries AD. You'll have to decide for yourself how well you think they've traveled . . .

An incompetent teacher was asked who Priam's mother was. As he didn't know the answer, he replied: "It's polite to call her Madam."

An incompetent astrologer cast a man's horoscope and told him: "You are unable to father children." When the man objected that he already had seven of them, the astrologer replied: "Well, you'd better look after them then!"

A man returned from a trip abroad and went to see an incompetent fortune-teller. He asked about his family. The fortune-teller replied: "Everyone is fine, especially your father." When the man objected that his father had been dead for a decade, the fortune-teller replied: "You obviously don't know who your real father is!"

Someone decided to tease a notorious joker. "I had sex with your wife, without paying a dime," he claimed. The joker replied: "It's my duty as a husband to sleep with that monstrosity. What's your excuse?"

An Abderite [i.e. a resident of the city of Abdera in Thrace, clearly a place not known for its intellectuals], saw a eunuch talking to a woman and asked if she was his wife. When the man explained that eunuchs can't have wives, the Abderite asked: "So is she your daughter then?"

A cheeky astrologer cast a sick boy's horoscope. After assuring the mother that the boy had many good years ahead of him, the astrologer demanded payment. "Come back tomorrow and I'll pay you," she said. "But what if the boy dies in the night and I lose my fee?" he replied.

John Pertwee – Soothsayer

Amanda Barrie – Cleopatra

Kenneth Williams – Julius Caesar
("Infamy! Infamy! They've all got it in for me!")

Francis de Wolff – Agrippa

Julie Stevens – Gloria

Sheila Hancock – Senna Pod

Joan Sims – Calpurnia

Jim Dale – Horsa

Charles Hawtrey – Seneca

Kenneth Connor – Hengist Pod

Sid James – Mark Anthony

STANSYK

Stansyk (c. 1480–1560), Poland's most famous court jester, served three of the country's monarchs: Alexander, Sigismund the Old, and Sigismund Augustus. In 1533, Sigismund the Old had a huge bear brought to him from Lithuania and released in a forest near Krakow for him to hunt. During the pursuit, the bear was cornered and then charged at the Royal Party. In the ensuing chaos, the queen fell off her horse, triggering a miscarriage.

After the incident, Sigismund summoned Stansyk and berated him for running away rather than attempting to fight off the bear. "It is a greater folly to let out a bear who was locked in a cage," replied the jester. This remark is often interpreted as an oblique reference to the king's policy towards Prussia, which Poland had recently conquered but neglected to incorporate into the kingdom.

J. D. BOGDANOFF

If you thought court jesters were a thing of the past, you'd be mistaken. In 1999, the King of Tonga issued a royal decree declaring a 44-year-old American named Jesse Bogdanoff "King of Jesters and Jester to the King, to fulfil his royal duty sharing mirthful wisdom and joy as a special goodwill ambassador to the world." Unfortunately, subsequent events would make the King look rather more foolish than his jester.

Bogdanoff first met King Taufa'ahau Tupou IV in 1994 while working for the Bank of America. He had discovered that the tiny Pacific nation had more than $20 million sitting dormant in a bank account, and travelled to Tonga to ask his client what he wanted to do with it. (The cash had been earned during the 1980s through the sale of passports to Hong Kong citizens.) Apparently the pair instantly hit it off, falling into a long conversation about the O. J. Simpson case.

Five years later, Bogdanoff decided to leave the Bank of America, but he wanted to keep the Tonga account, and the only way he could do it legally was by becoming an employee of the Tongan government. So he jumped into a plane and went to the King to ask for a job. As he was born on April 1, Bogdanoff suggested that court jester might be a suitable role. The King said he didn't need one, but the American prevailed after persuading him that the appointment would be good for tourism and PR.

Shortly after he became Tonga's official jester, Bogdanoff was appointed Financial Adviser to the government on a salary of $250,000 a year. He proceeded to invest the national fund, now worth $26 million, in a range of disastrous ventures, pre-eminently a life insurance company called Millennium Asset Management that went bankrupt in 2002. The Tongans lost nearly everything, and attempted to prosecute Bogdanoff for fraud. Two years later, the jester agreed to pay $1 million to the Tongan government to settle the case, with no admission of liability.

Pecunia non olet **(Money doesn't stink).**

Graffito at Pompeii

Stories about Nasrudin Hodja, a legendary mullah who managed to be both wise and idiotic at the same time, are told from China to West Africa. To Arabs, he is better known as Juha. Hodja is believed to have lived in Turkey during the 14th century and to have been a contemporary of Tamurlane the Great. There is a modern tomb dedicated to him in the Turkish town of Aksehir, and a statue of him sitting the wrong way round on a donkey in Bukhara in Uzbekistan.

It is difficult to be sure which of the many tales about Hodja are authentic, because his role as a proverbial trickster has ensured that almost any witty comment or deed gets ascribed to him in the end. But a few examples will give you the typical flavor:

Nasrudin was sitting on the bank of a river. A man on the other side shouted: "Hey, how do I get across?" "You are across," replied Hodja.

A man came to Hodja's house to try to borrow some money. Finding him repairing his roof, he called for him to come down. "Can you lend me some cash?" asked the neighbor. Hodja said nothing, but beckoned the man to follow him. Then he climbed the ladder and returned to the spot where he'd been working, along with his nonplussed neighbor. Then he leaned over and whispered in his ear: "I haven't got any!"

Someone asked Hodja which was more important to humanity, the Sun or the Moon. "The Moon of course!" said Hodja. "We need more light at night!"

One day Hodja wanted to go into town and leaped on his donkey in a hurry. His neighbors shouted "Hodja! You're facing the wrong way." "No I'm not," replied the mullah, who knew perfectly well where the town was. "It's the donkey who's facing the wrong way!'

I have other sons.

Lord Stanley's reply to Richard III in 1485 when the king threatened to execute his son George, Lord Strange

---

> **All right, but apart from the sanitation, medicine, education, wine, public order, irrigation, roads, the freshwater system and public health, what have the Romans ever done for us?**
> Reg, leader of the Judean People's Front (or is it the People's Front of Judea?) in *The Life of Brian*

JEFFREY HUDSON

Also known as "Lord Minimus," Jeffrey Hudson (1619–1682) was the diminutive fool of Queen Henrietta Maria, wife of Charles I. He was known as much for his tiny size as for his witty remarks. According to several contemporary accounts, Hudson was only 18 or 19 inches tall. He was also normally proportioned, in sharp contrast to the dwarves kept at many European courts of the era.

Hudson was introduced to Queen Henrietta shortly after his seventh birthday. The King and Queen were staying with the Duke of Buckingham, and a large pie was placed before them when they sat down for dinner. Jeffrey suddenly emerged from it clad in miniature armor. The young Queen was captivated by him and immediately took him into her service.

Hudson's career was packed with adventure. He fought with the Royalists during the English Civil War, and then fled to France in 1644 to join the Queen in exile. While there, he challenged a man to a duel and shot him in the head. This led to his dismissal from court. Shortly afterwards, Hudson was captured by Barbary pirates and sold into slavery in North Africa. He remained there for 25 years, only returning to England when a benefactor paid his ransom.

According to Scott Noegel, an associate professor in the Department of New Eastern Languages and Civilizations at the University of Washington, Ancient Egyptian humor fell into five categories.

Satire – this largely consisted of the depiction of important figures with unshaven or otherwise unflattering appearances. Egyptians loathed body hair.

Scatological jokes – defecating hyenas were particularly popular, as were pictures of people vomiting.

Sexual jokes – from innuendo to explicit depiction.

Slapstick – hammers landing on people's heads and boatloads of passengers being tipped into the Nile.

Animal-based humor – Noegel describes papyrus sketches showing "ducks pecking at someone's buttocks, baboons and cats out of control, animals riding on top of other unlikely animals, baboons playing instruments, and animals drinking and dining." One such sketch shows a mouse pharaoh charging at a group of cat warriors in a chariot pulled by two dogs. Another papyrus shows a lion beating an antelope in a game of chess.

In the beginning was the laugh . . . When God burst out laughing, there was light. When he burst out laughing the second time, the waters were born . . . At the seventh burst of laughter, the soul was born.

Egyptian papyrus, third century BC

THE FOOL'S ACCESSORIES

Inflated pigs' bladders · A marrotte, or mock sceptre · "Motley" clothing (i.e. composed of several materials) · Triple-pointed hats, representing the ears and tails of a donkey · Clothes made from the same material as the decoration in the employer's WC · Petticoats (for "natural" or mentally handicapped fools) · Cock's comb · False tail (in early times)

> ## A Cappadocian was bitten by a snake. The snake died.
>
> Ancient Greek joke about the residents of a province of Asia Minor

ARCHY ARMSTRONG

James I's jester Archy Armstrong first came to the King's attention as a pleading convict. The authorities had traced a sheep rustler operating on the border between England and Scotland to a lonely moorland cottage. When they burst into the premises, they found nobody there except an apparently half-witted lad rocking a cradle that presumably contained a younger relative. The men left, but returned on an intuition. They pulled back the covers of the cot to reveal a sheep.

Armstrong was arrested and taken to Jedburgh, where King James happened to be holding a justice-dispensing session. After he had been sentenced to death for sheep-stealing, Armstrong begged James to delay his execution. He claimed that he had only just heard of the Bible and wanted to read it before he died. When the King assented, the crafty young man announced: "Then Devil take me if I read a word of it as long as my eyes are open!" James was so impressed that he gave him a job on the spot.

UP POMPEII! CHARACTERS

The Roman setting of Frankie Howerd's innuendo-heavy 1970s sitcom allowed him to enjoy himself with character names. The following all appeared in the series—Biggus Dickus eat your heart out:

Colossa · Noxius
Hernia · Odius
Typhus · Umbilicus
Spurius · Lecherus
Scrubba · Bilius · Erotica

THE FEAST OF FOOLS

In cities all over medieval Europe, the weeks either side of Christmas were the cue for the established order to be turned on its head. The Feast of Fools kicked off on 6 December with the election of an altar boy or choirboy from the local cathedral as a "Boy Bishop." Three weeks and a day later, on the Feast of the Holy Innocents (the children supposedly massacred by King Herod), the youthful prelate would preach a sermon and preside over the liturgy.

On New Year's Eve, the Vespers service in the cathedral started off as normal, but when the words: "He has put down the mighty from their seats and exalted the humble" were spoken, the junior members of the clergy would start chanting: "Put them down! Put them down!" They would then swap seats with the senior priests who usually sat in more elevated pews.

The fun typically continued the following day with celebrations for the Feast of the Circumcision. These would begin with a donkey walking up the aisle of the cathedral carrying a young mother and baby on its back. During the mass that followed, the celebrant was expected to replace the regular text with brays at certain prescribed points. After ending the service with the words "Ita missae est" ("the mass has ended"), the priest would bray three times and the congregation would reply in kind.

> ## Yes please. Could you move out of my light?
>
> The Greek philosopher Diogenes, who lived in a barrel, when Alexander the Great visited him and asked if there was anything he wanted

NARCOLEPTIC WILL

Will Somers was the man charged with the dangerous job of keeping Henry VIII amused. The monarch acquired his services when his previous employer, Richard Farmor of Northamptonshire, was imprisoned for sending eight pence and a couple of shirts to a Catholic priest. There are various surviving pictures of Somers, who was also court jester to Henry's children Edward VI and Mary Tudor. There is a good example in the Royal Collection. Painted by an anonymous artist around 1445, *The Family of Henry VIII* depicts Somers walking about in a garden with a monkey on his back.

Somers' wit seems to have been predominantly verbal. When Henry complained of his lack of funds one day, Somers replied: "You have so many frauditors, conveyors, and deceivers that they get all to themselves" (he meant "auditors, surveyors, and receivers"). The thing that really made his contemporaries laugh, though, was his habit of nodding off at inopportune moments. He once fell asleep while clambering over a stile in Windsor Great Park. While he was dozing, a kind local woman tied him to it to prevent him falling off when he awoke. He was also said to "laye(s) him downe amongst the Spaniels to sleep" and to "stande all day yn slomber."

Double acts

TWO'S NOT JUST COMPANY,
IT'S TALENT SQUARED

Ronnie Corbett (the little one) and Ronnie Barker (the larger one) are accomplished comic performers in their own right (*Sorry, Open All Hours, Porridge*), but they clicked magnificently in their television series *The Two Ronnies*, which ran all through the 1970s and into the late 1980s.

The series involved a series of sketches (and usually at least one song) in which the men appeared in character, rather than as themselves (one way in which they differed from Morecambe and Wise). A favorite moment in each show was when Corbett had a solo spot, as himself, perched on an oversized chair, telling an apparently rambling and ad-libbed story than was actually carefully crafted and brought the winding theme to a conclusion with a sharp punch line.

Among their regular sketches, Charley Farley, the Victorian detective, was a popular feature, while on the Victorian theme, one of the most inventive and amusing was a conversation between Barker (as Edward Prince of Wales) and Corbett, with Corbett playing Queen Victoria—the twist was that the queen was convinced she was Jewish!

Like other comics before them (Burns and Allen on radio, and Rowan and Martin on television, both of them in the US), the Ronnies had a ritual farewell at the end of each episode, with Corbett saying: "It's good night from me," and Barker saying: "And it's good night from him." The double act came to an end with Barker's decision to retire in 1988, but at least the pair went out on a high.

> **Better an eternity in Hell with Little and Large . . . than a single "Christmas with the Osmonds."**
>
> Clive James

Shirley Bassey
Glamorous diva, she sang the
Goldfinger theme song

Glenda Jackson
1970s television and film star, now
a Member of Parliament

Vanessa Redgrave
Film star, beauty and
political activist

Laurence Olivier
First Sir, then Lord. Britain's most
distinguished actor

Elton John
Pop star and more recently writer
of stage and screen musicals

Cliff Richard
Eternally youthful pop star and
committed Christian

Burt Bacharach
King of cool composers, now
fashionable again

Diana Rigg
Sexy, leggy, classical actress,
Bond girl and Avenger

Angela Rippon
Ballet-trained newsreader who
showed off her legs in a classic
dance sequence

Vincent Price
"Camp King" of horror movies

Peter Cushing
"Wizened old Prince" of
horror movies

Michael Caine
Actor and restaurateur plagued by
the catchphrase: "Not many
people know that"

Harold Wilson
British Prime Minister (1964–1970,
1974–1976) and pipe smoker

Michael Parkinson
Talk-show presenter

**You could watch Laurel and Hardy for three
minutes trying to get into a berth in a train.**

Michael Richards, who played Cosmo Kramer in *Seinfeld*

VOTERS' CHOICE

The Channel 4 TV show *The Comedian's Comedian* asked 500 comics (in the UK and the US) for their 50 favorite comics. Double acts—and comedians best-known for being part of a double act—that scored highly were as follows:

Peter Cook (overall winner)

Eric Morecambe (4th)

Stan Laurel and Oliver Hardy (7th)

Vic Reeves and Bob Mortimer (9th)

Ronnie Barker (16th)

Dawn French and Jennifer Saunders (31st)

Eric Sykes (44th)

DUDLEY MOORE AND SIR JOHN GIELGUD

In the context of comic double acts, Dudley Moore is generally paired with Peter Cook, with whom he formed one of the great comic duos—on stage and on television—of the 1960s (*Pete 'n' Dud*). However a more interesting duo—albeit only in the cinema, and in the context of two films—is Dudley Moore and Sir John Gielgud.

Gielgud, a classic actor who excelled in Shakespeare, appeared in the two *Arthur* films with Dudley, playing his stiff-upper-lip English butler. The laughs were largely due to the contrast between his immaculate, very proper, very English appearance, the fact that audiences knew this was an immensely distinguished man of the theater, and the fact that the script called for him to use bad language. Such was the success of his performance that when he died, the passing of this unsurpassed Hamlet, this fabulous Richard II, this silver-voiced epitome of poetry was headlined, in an American tabloid: "Dudley Moore's Butler Dead."

HALE AND PACE – THE TWO RONS

Hale and Pace first met in the early 1970s, when they were both training to be teachers. They soon realized that being stand-up comics was more fun—and eventually far more profitable—than teaching PE to shivering children, so they formed a double act.

Their most remarkable characters are the two Rons, otherwise referred to as "The Management." East End heavies in dark suits, they owe a lot to the Krays (Ronnie and Reggie), although admirers of the Krays would be unlikely to enjoy the way the pair send up the psychotic violence of a certain brand of criminal.

ROWAN AND MARTIN

Rowan and Martin's *Laugh-In* ran from 1968 to 1973 and was not only an opportunity for America to enjoy two talented comedians, Dan Rowan and Dick Martin, but also a platform for other comic talents, including those of Goldie Hawn, who proved herself to be a comedienne in her own right as well as a Hollywood star.

The two signed off each week with a parody of the radio comedians George Burns and Gracie Allen, with Rowman saying: "Say Good night, Dick," and Martin replying: "Good night, Dick." Not exactly hilarious, but it was a catchphrase! Other sayings were: "I didn't know that!," "Go to your room!" and: "You bet your sweet bippy!"

Of the two, Martin was the boisterous buffoon, and Rowan the straight man. They encouraged satire as well as comedy, and in 1968 predicted (and the joke lay in its ludicrous implausibility) that Ronald Reagan would be President of the United States in 20 years' time . . .

Among those who had a break on their show were the bizarre 1960s singer Tiny Tim (who sang "Tip Toe Through the Tulips" on air), pop group the Bee Gees and comedienne Lily Tomlin.

kings of comedy

LONG-RUNNING DOUBLE ACTS

43 years Eric Morecambe and Ernie Wise (1941–1984)

27 years Stan Laurel and Oliver Hardy (1927–1954)

21 years Eric Sykes and Hattie Jacques (1959–1980)

18 years Dawn French and Jennifer Saunders (1987–present)

16 years Ronnie Barker and Ronnie Corbett (1971–1987)

10 years Dean Martin and Jerry Lewis (1946–1956)

MORECAMBE AND WISE – PUSHING UP THE PIGEONS?

There's been a long-running campaign in London to get a statue for the "spare" plinth in Trafalgar Square. At the moment the problem seems to have been solved by putting changing pieces of modern art on it, but there's still a debate. Should it be Nelson Mandela? How about the Queen Mother?

What about a comic? In one poll (in 1999), Eric Morecambe was voted "Comedian of the Century." Who better to stand, dancing, hand behind head, in his trademark gesture, than Morecambe's finest: he took his stage name after his hometown—his real name was Eric John Bartholomew.

Eric Morecambe was an avid birdwatcher in his spare time, and the statue to him that's been erected in Morecambe has a pair of binoculars slung round his neck. What better place for a birdwatcher than Trafalgar Square, which despite the best efforts of Mayor Ken, is still swarming with pigeons?

There ought to be some reflection of the fact that Morecambe will always be associated with Ernie Wise—perhaps one of Wise's toupees, about which Morecambe often joked ("Can you see the join?") lying at his feet would be an appropriate gesture.

DESTINED FOR (SEMI) GREATNESS

Since starting out as a 1999 HBO TV series of six short episodes, *Tenacious D* has become a long-term comedy and musical venture for its amiable masterminds, actor Kyle Gass and comedian Jack Black. The whole idea behind their act was to poke gentle fun at the rock fan mentality by creating two misfits who are so full of rock spirit that they have become legends in their own heads.

After the series, "the D" returned in 2001 with a self-titled album, which contained such memorable tunes as, "One Note Song," "Kyle Quit the Band," "Karate Schnitzel" and "Rock Your Socks"; along with other titles that are too rude to mention. They found genuine fame with their video for the song "Tribute," which told of their encounter with the Devil in the desert one night, and how they escaped his clutches by playing him The Best Song in the World—except that the song they're singing is only about The Song rather than The Song itself, and therefore just a "Tribute." Foo Fighter Dave Grohl played the Devil, MTV adored it, the album sold well and the D went on tour.

In 2005, Jack and Kyle started on their movie, *Tenacious D: The Pick of Destiny*. Meat Loaf plays Jack's father. The plot? "I run away from home because [Dad] doesn't understand the rock!" Jack explains. "And then I meet Kyle and we form Tenacious D and he runs me through a training program . . . And then we go on our first quest to be the greatest band on Earth!"

> **It's the saddest day of my life. I feel like I've lost a limb, I have been robbed of a partner and brother, there is a cold draught down one side of me where Eric should be.**
>
> Ernie Wise on Eric Morecambe's death

DEAN MARTIN AND JERRY LEWIS

Dean Martin and Jerry Lewis first worked together at the "500" club in Atlantic City in 1946, and had a stage and television partnership that lasted a decade, before finally splitting up. Both men were very successful comics who had a mutually complementary style: Martin was the suave, sophisticated half; Jerry Lewis was a hurricane of physical energy.

Despite this, Martin had had plenty of energy himself as a young man, being a professional boxer, among other jobs, before he got into show business. Both men had successful film careers—Lewis being as madcap as ever: "I've had a great success being a total idiot."

Martin's very popular Las Vegas nightclub act required him to appear slightly drunk on stage, and a glass of whiskey was invariably his prop, but in reality he was drinking tea or apple juice. The drunk persona was an act that created a slight but helpful distance between himself and his audience, something he had needed once he'd lost the reassuring presence and support of Lewis at his side on stage.

Martin went on to be one of the senior figures in the Rat Pack—an initially dismissive nickname given them by Lauren Bacall, but which stuck and which they came to enjoy. The leader of the pack, or Chairman of the Board, as he liked to be known, was Frank Sinatra. Other members were Peter Lawford and Sammy Davis Jr.

They all enjoyed a drink, but Martin was the man who officially revelled in his alcoholic status: "I feel pity for people who don't drink. They wake up in the morning and that's the best they're going to feel all day!"

> **If it weren't for Abbott and Costello, many of the wonderful burlesque routines which are a part of the American fabric would have been lost forever. They were giants of their time, who truly immortalized burlesque forever. Maybe that art form is largely lost, but I try and keep it alive in my own show.**
>
> Jerry Seinfeld on pioneering dynamic duo, Abbott and Costello

CARTOON CHEMISTRY

Saturday mornings and TV dinners wouldn't be the same without those cartoon capers and devilish double acts who, try as they might, just couldn't live without each other . . .

Tom and Jerry
Pink Panther and Inspector Clouseau
Dangermouse and Penfold
Ren and Stimpy
Roadrunner and Wiley Kyote
Bugs Bunny and Elmer Fudd
Top Cat and Benny
Yogi Bear and Boo Boo
Batfink and Karate
Kermit and Miss Piggy
Dastardly and Mutley

But as the theme tune from *The Simpsons* cartoon spin-off *The Itchy and Scratchy Show* proves, getting the laughs these days can be tough love . . .
"They fight, and bite,
They fight and bite and fight!
Fight fight fight, bite bite bite,
The Itchy and Scratchy Show!"

Dawn French and Jennifer Saunders met at drama school—the Central School of Speech and Drama, in London. They were part of the thriving alternative comedy scene in the 1980s, performing with *The Comic Strip* at the Comedy Store (other members included Peter Richardson, Ade Edmondson, Rick Mayall, Nigel Planer, Alexei Sayle and Robbie Coltrane). Spotted by Jeremy Isaacs, then running Channel 4, they were given their own series, in which they were presented as comic actors, in sketches, rather than the stand-up comics they had started out as.

Both French and Saunders have flourishing careers away from each other—Dawn French, who is married to comedian Lenny Henry, is best-known these days for her starring role in the TV sitcom *The Vicar of Dibley*, while Jennifer Saunders' greatest hit is the *Absolutely Fabulous* comedy TV series, co-starring Joanna Lumley and Julia Sawalha. This series began as a sketch on the *French and Saunders* show but took off in its own right to become the most fashionable show of the 1990s (ironic, given its attacks on the fashion world).

French and Saunders have the traditional bonus of being very different from each other physically, French having the fuller figure. Size played a part in two sketches from their series. In one, a takeoff of *Star Wars*, French is asked: "If you are a Jedi Knight, how come you got such big tits?" In another, taking the mickey out of impossibly thin ballerinas, Saunders, dressed as a dancer, says: "We're not anorexics, we just don't think eating's very clever."

Say "Good night Gracie"

George Burns to his wife Gracie Allen at the end of their shows. She is commonly thought to have replied "Goodnight Gracie," but Burns later claimed all she actually said was "Good night."

> My thing with Owen [Wilson] is, when you get to know him, you don't expect much, so you're never let down. We have a relationship where we enjoy making fun of each other. When we were doing press for *Starsky & Hutch*, we'd be telling the same stories over and over and over. At a certain point, he'd get on me about telling the same stories and make fun of me. But then he'd steal them! Literally, he'd do an interview and tell one of my stories as if it were his. That's, like, classic Owen for you.
>
> Ben Stiller on comedy partner Owen Wilson, in *Maxim* 2004

ON THE ROAD

Bob Hope and Bing Crosby—a winning combination of comedian and crooner—were getting footloose and fancy-free and spinning spiritual wisecracks well before Kerouac penned his famous tale. Their first screen pairing, *Road to Singapore* in 1940 found the boys sparring over the hand of the glamorous globetrotter Dorothy Lamour. The film was so successful, they returned in 1941 as carnival con men who get swindled themselves on safari in *Road to Zanzibar*. The now-fabled formula continued in 1942 in *Road to Morocco*, with Bob and Bing as a pair of shipwreck survivors who take a camel ride into a comedic Arabian Nights–style adventure. Until finally, the pair embarked on that many-a-wise-cracker's-Mecca, the *Road to Utopia*—proof indeed that "he who sitteth in heaven shalt laugh."

SO . . . WHO'S ON FIRST AGAIN?

Performed on the *Kate Smith Radio Hour* and in the 1940 movie classic *One Night in the Tropics*, "Who's on first?"—vaudeville duo Abbott and Costello's famous signature skit—boosted the morale of many a wartime cinema visit, and set the scene for barrel-loads of banter to come . . .

Abbott: Goofè Dean. Well, let's see, we have on the bags,
Who's on first, What's on second, I Don't Know is on third . . .
Costello: That's what I want to find out.
Abbott: I say Who's on first, What's on second, I Don't Know's on third.
Costello: Are you the manager?
Abbott: Yes.
Costello: You gonna be the coach too?
Abbott: Yes.
Costello: And you don't know the fellows' names?
Abbott: Well I should.
Costello: Well then who's on first?
Abbott: Yes.
Costello: I mean the fellow's name.
Abbott: Who.
Costello: The guy on first.
Abbott: Who.
Costello: The first baseman.
Abbott: Who.
Costello: The guy playing . . .
Abbott: Who is on first!
Costello: I'm asking YOU who's on first.
Abbott: That's the man's name.
Costello: That's who's name?
Abbott: Yes.
Costello: Well go ahead and tell me.
Abbott: That's it.
Costello: That's who?
Abbott: Yes.

Money and politics

POLITICIANS? BANKERS?
YOU'VE GOT TO LAUGH

Launched in 1984, *Spitting Image* employed wickedly caricatured puppets to poke fun at politicians, both in the UK and abroad. Who can forget the saga of President Reagan's brain (and whether he would ever find it?) or the demolition job they did on David Steel (then a major politician, now a footnote in history, kicked upstairs to the House of Lords), whose career never really recovered from his depiction as a little glove puppet sticking out of the pocket of his political partner David Owen (then a major politician, now . . .).

Their major target, however, was always Margaret Thatcher, and in the days when British politics was dominated by larger-then-life characters—Thatcher, Norman Tebbit (represented as a leather-jacketed boot boy) and Michael Heseltine (slightly mad, and wearing an army camouflage jacket)—they had a field day.

In real life, Thatcher admired and hoped to be compared to Winston Churchill (the Falklands War being her equivalent of the Second World War). *Spitting Image* duly showed her dressed in a suit and waving a cigar. They also caught her voice, giving her two tones; one soft, feminine and cajoling, the other deep, masculine and threatening.

One sketch in particular summed up her relationship with her colleagues better than acres of political commentary in the press: at a restaurant, where the Cabinet are dining, the waiter asks Thatcher what she'll eat. She replies: "Beef." "And the vegetables?" asks the waiter. Thatcher looks disparagingly round the table. "They'll have the same!"

The show ran for 14 years, and was merciless to John Major (portrayed by a totally grey puppet with a penchant for peas) as well as to his rival, Neil Kinnock ("Kinnochio"). But with Thatcher's political death in November 1990, the fun and the fizzle went out of the program and it was wound up. However, Tony Blair did appear in the last few series—as a grinning puppet "puppet" hypnotized by Peter Mandelson's snake.

> **It's morally wrong to allow a sucker to keep his money.**
> W. C. Fields

OPEN ALL HOURS—SHOPPING FOR LAUGHS

As Joan Rivers always reminds us, retail therapy is good for the soul—even if you lost yours years ago:

Are You Being Served?
Who can forget Mr Humphries' enthusiasm for taking inside leg measurements, or the constant tribulations of Mrs Slocombe's pussy?

Open All Hours
Ronnie Barker and David Jason (then a mere support actor) keeping the shop open late and an eye on Lynda Barron's marrows . . .

The League of Gentlemen
Royston Vasey's local shop, run by Edward and Tubbs Tattsyrup, is the last place you'd want to wander into when you've broken down.

The Two Ronnies **General Store**
Parker's bumpkin customer drives Corbett's proprietor to distraction with ambiguous requests for hardware. Four candles becomes "fork handles" and so on.

> **I have enough money to last me the rest of my life, unless I buy something.**
> Jackie Mason, Rabbi and comic

BEN ELTON AND BLACKADDER

Ben Elton's 1980s catchphrase— "Ooh, little bit of politics there!"— reflected the fact that his alternative comedy style was born and fashioned in the Thatcher years, when money became the center of every conversation, usually on the subject of house prices. In the era of Yuppies and triumphant Conservatism, Elton provided an intelligent and perceptive critical voice.

While not everyone thought his stand-up quite as funny as he evidently did (his own laughter was often the cue for the audience's), Elton was a wonderful comedy writer. His partnership with Richard Curtis (of *Notting Hill* fame) reached its peak with the *Blackadder* series. The comedy poked fun at the Establishment in the broadest sense, taking the mickey out of several centuries of big cheeses, from Queen Elizabeth I to barking mad First World War generals.

Here, echoing a classic 1960s sketch by Bob Newhart, Blackadder expresses his disgust (and envy) at Sir Walter Raleigh's triumphant return from America:
Blackadder: "Bloody explorers, ponce off to Mumbo-Jumbo land, come home with a tropical disease, a suntan and a bag of brown lumpy things, and

Bob's your uncle, everyone's got a picture of them in lavatory."

Ben, who is related to the historian Lord Elton, had a gist for delivering left-wing political tirades while demonstrating his erudition (and adding to other people's) in a light-hearted way.

The *Blackadder* scripts were so witty that they swept viewers along with them whatever their political persuasion. Thus a whole generation of right-wingers, who wouldn't have dreamed of attending Elton's live sessions, happily sat down to watch several series of *Blackadder* that ridiculed the monarchy, the aristocracy, the public-school system and the armed forces' officer class.

In one episode, Blackadder joins the Royal Flying Corps and finds its officers even more dementally hearty than the ones in the trenches:
Lieutenant George: "Crikey! I'm looking forward to today. Up-diddly-up, down-diddly-down, whoops-poop, twiddly-dee—a decent scrap with the fiendish Red Baron—a bit of a jolly old crash landing behind enemy lines—capture, torture, escape and then back home in time for tea and medals."

Lenny Bruce, who died of an overdose a couple of months before his 41st birthday, was an internationally-known (and banned) stand-up comedian who revolutionized his profession, turning comedy into a serious political tool.

He was brought to trial several times, suffered constant police persecution and was blackballed by many club owners who couldn't face the hassle that came with employing him. But although Bruce's "crimes" were ultimately political, the authorities had to rely on issues of taste to get him. He was prosecuted for obscenity for using four-letter words that many would now see as unexceptionable. He turned this prosecution (which most people thought of as straightforward persecution) into a stream of highly political tirades against the state of American culture.

Bruce appealed to the liberal Hollywood set, and in 1974 his life story was turned into a film. *Lenny* starred Dustin Hoffman, while alternative comedian (and wearer of women's clothes and makeup) Eddie Izzard played Bruce in the 1990s' stage show of the same name.

Changing morals and political climate eventually led to the Governor of New York, George Pataki's decision, in 2003, to posthumously pardon Bruce for his obscenity conviction.

Themes that Bruce played on included his Jewishness, early poverty and his distaste for the Roman Catholic Church. These examples should give the general idea:

"A lot of people say to me: 'Why did you kill Christ?' 'I dunno . . . it was one of those parties, got out of hand, you know.' We killed him because he didn't want to become a doctor, that's why we killed him!"

"I won't say ours was a tough school, but we had our own coroner. We used to write essays like: What I'm going to be if I grow up."

"If Jesus had been killed 20 years ago, Catholic school children would be wearing little electric chairs around their necks instead of crosses."

The jokes were good, but it was Bruce's general daring, his pushing of boundaries and his left-wing ideals that have made him such an icon to subsequent generations of comedians and actors.

> **All I ask is the chance to prove that money can't make me happy.**
>
> Spike Milligan

DODD DIN'T DIDDLE

Ken Dodd's 1989 trial for alleged tax evasion saw many of the big names in showbiz line up to defend him. Public sympathy firmly behind him, he still took the precaution of hiring as his defense lawyer George Carman, QC—of whom fellow comic Barry Cryer observed: "That man would get Hitler off!" Dodd admitted that he had huge stashes of cash at home, which he periodically took to offshore bank accounts—as you do.

At one point things looked pretty hairy for our Ken. Cryer quipped that prisoners at the local jail had strung out a banner that read: "Coming Next Week—Ken Dodd!" Fortunately he was cleared of any intentional wrongdoing and returned to what he did best—touring the country, breaking records for the lengths of runs, and wielding his legendary tickle stick ("People say it's a Freudian symbol, but it's a fallacy!")

The trial may have been a great strain—"I haven't had a happy day for years," Dodd confessed in an interview—but it gave him a whole new line of gags for his act: "Do you remember when income tax was only three shillings in the pound? Trouble is, I thought it still was!"

> **Strange women lying in ponds distributing swords is no basis for a system of government.**
>
> Dennis in *Monty Python and the Holy Grail*

One of America's (and the world's) richest comics, Bob Hope was born in straightened circumstances in England in 1903, moving to the US in 1907. From the safety of a position of wealth, he joked about the family's early poverty. "Looking back at my Cleveland boyhood, I know now that it was grim going," he wrote. "But nobody told us Hopes it was grim. We just thought that's the way things were. We had fun with what we had. We ate regularly, although sometimes when we'd eaten everything on the table, we sat there staring hungrily at each other."

As an adult, Hope made full use of his income from stand up and comedy acting. He invested skilfully, owning several oil wells and so much prime Californian property that Humphrey Bogart once complained: "every time I see a piece of land I like I find out Bob Hope owns it!"

Hope was also known for his patriotism, and entertained troops in combat zones in the Second World War, the Korean War and in Vietnam. He was on good terms with many presidents: John F Kennedy gave him a Congressional medal. Accepting the honor, Hope said: "Thank you, Mr. President. I feel very humble, but I think I have the strength of character to fight it."

He was also happy to work with the Republicans, and in the 1980s, during Reagan's heyday, he had a cultural center named after him. Referring to a notoriously randy Democrat presidential candidate, he said: "Naming a cultural center after me is like naming a monastery after Gary Hart!"

> ## I told the Inland Revenue I didn't owe them a penny because I lived near the seaside.
>
> Ken Dodd

Fans of *Punch*—the now defunct British magazine of social humor and political satire—may have noticed that some of the captions or cartoons read as if they were created by a drunken committee. While the magazine employed the services of some of the most witty and irreverent voices in the world, the now infamous *Punch* Lunch provided just the right atmosphere to "help things along." For the 150 years of its publication, the founders of the magazine held its staff meetings over dinner—at first at Ludgate Pub and from 1855 at a specially commissioned *Punch* Table in the magazine offices. When *Punch* moved to a new building 10 years later, the publication was awarded with its own banqueting hall.

The highlight of the meal was to discuss the contents of the main political cartoon as the brandy was passed around. The editor would call "Gentlemen, the Cartoon" and one of the writers would then proffer some ridiculous suggestion such as "Disraeli in the style of a sphinx." The unfortunate artist then had to do the best job he could! In light of the fact that some of the cartoons and captions looking like they had been cobbled together by a table full of drunks, it was agreed to move the tradition to before lunch. This went on until 1969 when editor William Davis decided he didn't want part of his magazine edited at the meal table.

The lunch was also an opportunity for staff and regular contributors to meet outside guests, including writers, artists, politicians, business people, showbiz celebrities and even the occasional member of the Royal family.

Famous diners included Norman Tebbit, introduced as "the person" least likely to be served in a Chinese takeaway; Margaret Thatcher, the first female UK Prime Minister and indeed the first woman at the previously men-only table; a young Prince Charles, who like other guests carved his initials into the table but whose detective said "My God, you've certainly had trouble with vandals"; former British PM Edward Heath; the Duke of Edinburgh; P. G. Wodehouse; and Sir John Betjeman. Unfortunately the magazine closed in 2002, perhaps as a result of the extortionate booze, food and cigar bill!

Rapping trickster Ali G alias Sacha Baron Cohen got some fast food answers with all the trimmings from three times US Presidential Candidate and right-wing politician Patrick Buchanan when he took the *Ali G Show* **stateside. Unless Buchanan was the only politician brave enough to acknowledge that BLTs were in fact America's biggest weapon of mass self-destruction . . .**

Ali G: "Does you think that Saddam ever was able to make these weapons of mass destruction or whatever, or as they is called, BLTs?"

Patrick Buchanan: "The—was Saddam able to make them?"

Ali G: "Could he make BLTs?"

Buchanan: "Yes. At one time, he was using BLTs on the Kurds in the north. If he had anthrax, if he had mustard gas . . ."

Ali G: "Whatever he put in them."

Buchanan: "No. No, no. If he had mustard gas, no."

Ali G: "Let's say he didn't have mustard and the BLTs just was plain. Would you have been able to go in there then?"

Buchanan: "No."

Sacha Baron Cohen later suggested to *The Times* that Buchanan may have thought he was referring to "ballistic long-range trajectory missiles."

> If only God gave me a clear sign:
> like making a large deposit in my name
> at a Swiss bank.
>
> Woody Allen

PROPELLED TO FAME AND FORTUNE

The 1970s British television show *New Faces*, presented by Derek Hobson, was a way into the limelight and wealth for many performers, including a fair few comedians:

Lenny Henry
animated black comedian and television presenter
from the West Midlands

Jim Davidson
Jack the lad Cockney comedian

Victoria Wood
statuesque comedienne, one of the highest-earning
women entertainers in Britain

Joe Pasquale
bubbly comic with a high-pitched voice

Michael Barrymore
physically out of the Cleese mold, but not much to
laugh about in his life recently

Les Dennis
Comedian, impressionist, soap actor, and presenter of *Family Fortunes*

Some of the best lines from the US President . . .

You see, not only did the attacks help accelerate a recession, the attacks reminded us that we are at war.
On the September 11 attacks, Washington DC, June 8, 2005

It's in our country's interests to find those who would do harm to us and get them out of harm's way.
Washington DC, April 28, 2005

Who could have possibly envisioned an erection—an election in Iraq at this point in history?
Washington, DC, January 10, 2005

Justice ought to be fair.
White House Economic Conference, Washington DC, December 15, 2004

The truth of that matter is, if you listen carefully, Saddam would still be in power if he were the president of the United States, and the world would be a lot better off.
Second presidential debate, St. Louis, October 8, 2004

I'm not the expert on how the Iraqi people think, because I live in America, where it's nice and safe and secure.
Washington DC, September 23, 2004

We actually misnamed the war on terror. It ought to be the Struggle Against Ideological Extremists Who Do Not Believe in Free Societies Who Happen to Use Terror as a Weapon to Try to Shake the Conscience of the Free World.
Washington DC, August 6, 2004

Our enemies are innovative and resourceful, and so are we. They never stop thinking about new ways to harm our country and our people, and neither do we.
Washington DC, August 5, 2004

Then you wake up at the high school level and find out that the illiteracy level of our children are appalling.
Washington DC, January 23, 2004

Just remember it's the birds that's supposed to suffer, not the hunter.
Advising quail hunter and New Mexico Senator, Pete Domenici, Roswell, NM, January 22, 2004

So thank you for reminding me about the importance of being a good mom and a great volunteer as well.
St. Louis, Missouri, January 5, 2004

WE SHALL NOT BE OVERRULED

Although initial airings of the satirical news series *That was the Week That Was* had punters gagging for more, the BBC—worried about offending prominent politicians and influential figures—attempted to limit the activities of the team by scheduling follow-up repeats of the television series *The Third Man* so the potential antagonists could not overrun their slot. Presenter David Frost however—not one to be outwitted by anyone—took to reading out detailed synopses of *The Third Man* plots of the following *The Third Man* episode at the end of each show, revealing all the twists and details so there was little point in anybody watching them. The BBC quickly dropped the repeats, and *That Was the Week That Was* was left open-ended once more. Unfortunately the series didn't return in 1964 as it was felt that the commentary would unduly affect the election. It did, however, trigger copycat shows in the US, Canada and Holland— the host of which, once the Netherland's most popular presenter, was eventually forced to leave because of escalating levels of hate mail. If only as many people listened to politicians, wrote to their MP or turned out to vote!

> ## I don't make jokes. I just watch the
> ## government and report the facts.
> Will Rogers, turn of the century vaudeville comedian, lasso
> throwing world record holder and joke US presidential
> candidate in 1928

The surrealists

COMEDY TAKEN THAT EXTRA STEP

> Tim: We are The Goodies . . .
> Bill and Graeme: Yes, we know that.
> Tim: . . . and we are . . . uh . . . going to do good to people.
> Bill: How wet.
>
> The Goodies

JOHN CLEESE – COMEDY IS SERIOUS BUSINESS

John Cleese—Python, Basil Fawlty, star of *Clockwise* and *A Fish Called Wanda*—is a best-selling author, a writer and performer of genius, and a very successful businessman. He has made millions from Video Arts, a company he and several others set up in the early 1970s to provide videos for training purposes.

His interest in making money from comedy was a source of some tension between him and his fellow Pythons, most of who had a very 1960s attitude to money—the pursuit of lucre was seen as a sell-out to capitalism and distinctly uncool.

There was also a very English (and middle class) attitude to money here—as Cleese has said, in England having money is perfectly all right; it's getting it that is considered vulgar . . .

Cleese himself went to public school—Clifton College, in Bristol—and many of his contemporaries have turned out to be accountants. Ironic, given the way the Pythons laid into the profession in many of their sketches.

The sales of Video Arts training films have kept Cleese's accountants happy for years, even if he may be—as one interviewer described him in *The Washington Post*—"Jack Benny with a BBC accent." At least (to paraphrase Liberace) he can laugh all the way to the bank.

SMELLY CAT

If Ross was the nerdy one, Monica the neurotic one and Joey the stupid one, Phoebe Buffay (Lisa Kudrow) was most definitely the surreal member of the cast of *Friends*. A psychic massage therapist, she sometimes supplemented her income by busking. Her most popular song was "Smelly Cat," which she once performed in a duet with Chrissie Hynde:

Smelly cat, smelly cat,
What are they feeding you?
Smelly cat, smelly cat,
It's not your fault.

They won't take you to the vet,
You're obviously not their favorite pet.
You may not be a bed of roses,
And you're no friend to those with noses.

DANNY LA RUE

La Rue is Britain's best-known female impersonator. As he says of himself: "I'm not a star, darling, I'm a legend!" And legends don't come much more surreal than this 6ft man who, sweeping on to a stage dressed in elaborate Edwardian women's clothes, greets the audience with a wink and the phrase, "Wotcha mates!"(delivered in an exaggeratedly deep voice).

These days he looks more like a glamorous granny than the sex bomb he used to be able to play, but he still packs them in. His act consisting of music hall outfits and timeless one-liners, which though aimed at a family audience are deliciously daring—well, for the old dears, anyway (old ladies seem to make up a large percentage of his fans).

La Rue was born in Ireland, and once he had become famous, he returned there. Standing on the stage in a figure-hugging frock, blazing with diamonds, his arm swept theatrically around the auditorium, taking in the audience as if to hug them: "When I left Ireland," he said, "I was wearing shorts and a shirt and blazer. Look what the English have done to me!"

Princesses only kiss frogs in fairy tales—and even then the kiss transforms them into handsome princes. In real life, it's not supposed to happen. But this didn't put off Peter Sellers, one of the greatest British comic talents of the 20th century.

He's known to most people (especially American audiences) for his roles in the *Pink Panther* movies, and for playing the simple gardener in *Being There*. To British fans of a certain age, however, he's best-known for his role as one of the surreal group of comics collectively known as the Goons, who flourished on radio from 1951 to 1960.

The 1950s and 1960s were the heyday of Princess Margaret, the Queen's younger sister, whose combination of beauty (at least until middle age, when she suddenly got plump and matronly), sex drive and royal status was irresistible to Peter Sellers, a boy from a modest background, who used his comic talent to acquire wealth, fame and beautiful women. He had a long-standing crush on the Princess, who liked him because he made her laugh (it can't have been his money she was after). Their friendship, which began when they were introduced by Alec Guinness, was rumored to be more than just platonic, but whatever the mechanics, the engine that drove it was comedy. The Princess made a rare appearance in a comic home movie: Sellers, standing before a coffin, announces that he will now do his impersonation of Princess Margaret. Then he disappears behind a cloth, and a few seconds later out comes . . . Princess Margaret.

After Sellers' death in 1980, Harry Secombe, interviewed on the television, said: "Peter was never very lucky with his ladies," and the Princess was no exception. Her only comment on his demise was that he was: "The most difficult man I ever knew."

I told you a million times, do not exaggerate.

Rick, *The Young Ones*

SPIKE MILLIGAN – PRINCE CHARLES'S JESTER

When not listening to the brass bands on the Buckingham Palace forecourt, or Mummy's Highland Piper's morning performances, Prince Charles grew up listening to the Goons. For a young man brought up in the rigid formality of court life, their anarchic humor had an understandable appeal, and Spike Milligan was a particular favorite of the Prince.

They met on many occasions over the years and the Prince, whose attitude to people is usually as formal as his dress, allowed Milligan a sort of court jester status.

Milligan, who suffered from recurring manic depression, pushed the boundaries of this relationship as far as they could go, and on one occasion a little bit further. At the British Comedy Awards ceremony in 1994, on being given a Lifetime Achievement Award, the presenter read out a warm letter of congratulations from Prince Charles. "Oh, the groveling little bastard!" said Milligan. He later faxed the prince, asking: "I suppose a knighthood is out of the question now?"

He may have resisted the "comedian" tag, preferring to call himself a performance artist, but New York's Andy Kaufman was a riot. Straining the goodwill of audiences with absurd acts, Kaufman surprisingly found favor in his early days with the kind of hard-bitten impresarios who'd fostered the careers of more conventional gag-merchants. Perhaps it was because they had seen so many approaches so many times that they found something in Kaufman to refresh the palate. One thing's for sure, though: he knew how to baffle. Here are a few of his more egregious moments.

Eating raw potatoes onstage for no apparent reason

Nodding off in a sleeping bag in front of paying crowds

Acting as a hopeless foreign comic before lurching into an Elvis routine

Launching the 1978 College Sex Concert Tour, the purpose of which was to help him fornicate with young girls who'd sent him fan mail

Creating an alternative persona, the lounge singer, Tony Clifton, who attacked Kaufman for using him to get rich

Taking an entire audience at Carnegie Hall to have post-show milk and cookies in a fleet of hired buses

Inaugurating, and then winning, the Inter-Gender Wrestling Championship by turning up at wrestling contests and offering $1,000 to any woman who could pin him down

Kaufman died in 1984, aged 35.
There is no record of him ever attending therapy.

Occupying territory somewhere between performance art and *Candid Camera*, Dom Joly's *Trigger Happy TV* (first shown in 2000) introduced British audiences to a new genre of television comedy. The essence of the show was to expose members of the public to bizarre staged incidents that appeared to be spontaneous. Thus a man might walk down a busy street wearing a dog costume and suddenly be attacked by a similarly attired mugger. Or a young, healthy traffic warden (played by the enormous Joly) might timidly approach an old lady and ask her to help him over the road.

Like many successful comedies of the early 21st century (*The Office, Ali G*), *Trigger Happy TV* got much of its mileage from making viewers cringe. The show ruthlessly exploited the good nature of its "victims," but somehow managed to be profoundly human at the same time. Its pathos-packed sketches could be strangely moving, and the program held up a revealing mirror to society. You can learn a lot about a culture from the way its members react to men screaming into giant mobile phones in art galleries, as any Brit who watches the American version will find, and vice-versa.

> ### I was doing some decorating, so I got out my step-ladder. I don't get on with my real ladder.
>
> Harry Hill, meandering British comedian who chucked his career as a doctor in favor of stand up. Thank God, given how weird he is.

Kenneth Williams is best known for his film roles in the *Carry On* series, from the 1950s to the 1980s. But the surreal side of his comedy came through not in these scripted film roles, but in his one-man appearances on radio, television and stage. He made his name in 1950s revues like *Pieces of Eight*, written by Peter Cook.

Cook wrote a classic sketch with Oedipal overtones in *One Over the Eight* (1961). Set in a barbershop, it drew on Williams's own background. Williams's father, who had been an unsympathetic presence in his early years, had been a barber. He was also a straightlaced one who loathed "poofs." Imagine his delight when little Kenneth came along.

The sketch had Cook as the customer and Williams as the barbershop proprietor—doing his usual flared nostrils, camp-as-Christmas but pretending-to-be-otherwise routine.

The customer asks for a trim. The barber, offended, wants to give him something much more elaborate: "You don't come into my little boutique to 'have a bit off.' You come in here to have it styled. I'm an *artiste de cheveux*. I'm a poet, a poet of the hair."

The customer becomes increasingly suspicious as the barber witters on about tints and waves: "I don't want any of this modern continental rubbish," to which Williams replies: "You call that continental! Poof! I say to that . . . I have boxers in here, all-in wrestlers . . . bishops, great burly men, they all come in here for a wave and a tint . . ."

The customer is worried he'll look "chi chi" and the barber, using "poof" as an exclamation (and digging the knife into Williams's father) says: "Chi chi? You know what I say to that, if anyone says that to me? Poof, I say. Poof, poof to them . . ." He then tells the customer that a heavyweight boxing champion used to come in and get smothered in Chanel and talcum powder: "Old Jack Schmelling. You wouldn't call him effeminate, would you? Poof, I say. He never went near a woman, never touched a woman in his life. There was nothing effeminate about Jack . . ."

The customer, appalled, insists on leaving, saying: "I'm not going out of here looking like a woman," and gets up, revealing he's wearing a kilt! The skit works well in its own right, but knowing Williams's background gives it that extra layer of bite, proving that revenge is a dish best eaten cold . . .

> **Surrealism had a great effect on me because then I realized that the imagery in my mind wasn't insanity. Surrealism to me is reality.**
>
> John Lennon

THE GOODIES — GONE TO OTHER THINGS

Monty Python was the surreal British comedy series that made the biggest splash in the 1970s, in the US as well as England, but, although they have less street cred, *The Goodies* were also wildly popular during the same era.

A trio of contrasting types—patriotic old Wykehamist Tim Brooke-Taylor; cynical, stroppy, scruffy Bill Oddie and absentminded boffin Graeme Garden—they banded together to tackle an array of bizarre threats, ranging from a giant kitten to an invasion of Rolf Harris clones (the then popular Australian artist).

There was an element of slapstick reminiscent of the silent movie era, and a gentleness noticeably absent from the *Monty Python* series. They appealed to a wide age range, but as the BBC wanted to show them at an early hour, they never really had the chance to use more adult material.

The Goodies ran on the BBC for a decade from 1970 before the show was transferred to ITV for its final year. Bill Oddie ended up as the most successful (in television terms, anyway) of the three post-Goodies, becoming a very popular presenter of wildlife programs, reflecting his passion for birds.

"The opera ain't over 'til the fat lady sings" as the saying goes, but with (Sir) Harry Secombe it was a case of the fat guy singing.

Secombe had a fine operatic tenor voice, but was better-known for making farting noises, during his time with the madcap Goons. As he once said: "Anyone who, for 25 years, has built a career on such tenuous foundations as a high-pitched giggle, a raspberry and a sprinkling of top 'Cs' needs all the friends he can get."

In fact Secombe had lots of friends, partly because of his talent as a comedian, partly because he was a genuinely nice guy and partly because he never seemed to take himself seriously. "I suffer fools gladly because I'm one myself," he once said.

The world tends to associate opera singers with large fat men, and Secombe certainly fitted the bill, making a career as a comic partly out of his figure, until heart problems in the 1970s persuaded him to lose weight.

He was in the rare position of being equally able to make a living from comedy or from music, and starred in several major shows, including the film version of Lionel Bart's *Oliver!* and the stage version of *The Pickwick Papers*. It was from this show that he had one of his two major hit singles: "If I Ruled The World" in 1963. The other major hit was: "This Is My Song" in 1967. He said, of his singing: "My voice is not so much 'bel canto' as 'can belto,'" and he belted his way into the hearts of British audiences from the 1940s to his last television appearances in the 1980s. Secombe died in 2001.

> ## Right, let's take a vote. Who gave the best presents this year?
>
> Competitive Dad, *The Fast Show*

SONG FOR EUROPE

In one memorable episode of *Father Ted,* Ted is goaded into attempting to write a song for the Eurovision Song Contest. Along with Dougal he creates "My lovely horse" . . .

Where are you going with your fetlocks blowing in the wind?
I want to shower you with sugarlumps,
And ride you over fences,
Polish your hooves every single day,
And bring you to the horse dentist,

My lovely horse,
You're a pony no more,
Running around with a man on your back,
Like a train in the night,
Like a train in the night.

FLANDERS AND SWAN – SURREAL SONGMASTERS

Michael Flanders and Donald Swann were a British duo who specialized in creating a strange, little world of their own. They did this on stage, in revues like *At The Drop Of A Hat*, which opened in Notting Hill in December 1956, and The Fortune Theatre, where their show ran for two years before going on an international tour to Europe, Canada and the US.

Unlike most comics, who actually use the stage—even if the microphone stand is their only prop—both men remained seated during their performances, Swann on the piano stool and Flanders in a wheelchair, to which he had been confined ever since contracting polio during the war.

Some of their songs were gently satirical, like the hit single "The Gasman Cometh"—a catalogue of the disasters inflicted on household by a succession of incompetent British workmen (Thank God they all seem to be Polish nowadays). Others like "The Gnu Song" were completely surreal: "I'm A Gnu. How do you do?" Among the wilder shores of songwriting inspiration visited by the pair was "First and Second Law," a ditty about thermodynamics.

The Laughing Policeman
Charles Penrose recorded this song, with an irritatingly catchy laughing
sequence as the chorus, back in 1926. Ooh ha ha ha ha!

Carry On Constable
Carry On police caper notable for a cameo appearance by Joan Hickson
(30 years later she was the definitive Miss Marple)

"Nick-Nick"
Catchphrase of the police character created by "Mr. P. C." Jim Davidson

Pink Panther
Immortal series of films starring Peter Sellers as bumbling Inspector Clouseau

The Thin Blue Line
Ben Elton's TV sitcom set in a police station

Not the Nine O'Clock News
Griff Rhys Jones's unreconstructed copper is upbraided for continually
arresting a Mr Winston Kodogo, essentially for being black

When people in Britain want to buy a pet,
they go to a pet shop. If they want to buy a
pet shop, they go to a pet shop shop. If they
want to buy a pet shop shop, well, they're just
being silly.

Narrator, *Little Britain*

Silence was golden

WHEN LAUGHTER FILLED
THE SOUND OF SILENCE

Sir Charles Chaplin was the biggest star of the silent movie era, a comic performer of genius, who increasingly combined pathos with humor, making his "Little Tramp" the best-loved figure in cinema history.

Chaplin was very keen on love in his private life, being married four times and fathering 11 children. Today his taste in wives would raise eyebrows—his first two wives were only 16 when he married them, and his fourth was 17 (Oona O'Neill, daughter of playwright Eugene O'Neill, who was less than thrilled at having his teenage daughter marry a white-haired 54-year-old). His third wife was a relatively ancient 25.

This taste for young girls was also reflected in *Limelight*, the 1952 feature film in which Chaplin plays an aging performer who rescues a young ballerina (Claire Bloom) from suicide. Although he thinks she should be off with a boy of her own age it is he who she loves—clearly a Chaplin fantasy. Other than that the film is actually very good, and Chaplin not only wrote, directed and starred in it, he also composed the haunting theme music. For silent movie lovers there's a moment of screen history when Chaplin and Buster Keaton, arguably the two greatest stars of that era, are reunited in the film as a (silent) double act.

> **He had occasional flashes of silence that made his conversation perfectly delightful.**
> Sydney Smith (Regency wit and supposedly the funniest man in England)

BUSTER KEATON – YOU'RE NEVER TOO YOUNG TO START

The thinking man's favorite silent movie star, Buster Keaton was an amazingly acrobatic performer whose physical daring, combined with his eternally wistful face, made him one of the most entertaining comic performers of the silent era.

Keaton learned his physical skill at an early age. His parents worked in vaudeville and performed a regular sketch about child rearing, in which young Buster (who started at the age of three) deliberately teases his musician father, until his father loses his temper and throws him about the stage—into the scenery, against walls and on occasion into the orchestra pit.

Even in the 1870s, this raised concerns about the treatment of children, but young Buster loved it. He learned, at a remarkably young age, that the more serious he looked as he was hurtling through the air, the more the audience laughed. The result was the deadpan face that amused audiences throughout the silent movie era.

Buster got his nickname (he was born Joseph Frank Keaton) from his godfather—the great escapologist Harry Houdini. Houdini saw the boy tumble down a flight of stairs without hurting himself and called him Buster (slang for a fall). The name stuck, and is now regularly used as a first name in the US.

Billy Wilder's 1950 film *Sunset Boulevard*—the inspiration for Andrew Lloyd Webber's 1980s musical—featured a deranged silent movie star living in a vast, decaying mansion on Sunset Boulevard. She takes in a down-on-his-luck writer and turns him into her toyboy.

The part of Norma Desmond was a fabulous, achingly camp one that has entertained generations of movie goers, and still represents the epitome of silent movie acting (all over-the-top gestures and insane theatricality). Yet it proved surprisingly hard to cast. Mae West was the original choice—and they don't get much camper than that—but she decided she was too young to play an ex-silent movie star.

Next, a real relic of the era, Pola Negri, furiously rounded on Wilder for suggesting she could possible play a has-been—though she was more washed up than a canteen of cutlery. In any case, during her tirade against him he decided her European accent was too strong. An approach to "America's sweetheart," Mary Pickford, produced more shrieks of outrage. Fortunately another director (George Cukor) suggested Gloria Swanson, the woman who had been Paramount Studios' biggest star in the 1920s.

The only thing she objected to was a screen test: "Don't you realize? I built Paramount!" she snapped. The line, slightly amended, became part of the movie when, having consented to a test, she was given the part and entered cinema history.

> ## Do not the most moving moments of our lives find us all without words?
>
> Marcel Marceau

HAROLD LLOYD – CLOCKING IT

One of the most enduring images of the silent movie era is of Harold Lloyd hanging from the hands of a clock, high above a busy street, in the aptly-named 1923 film *Safety Last*. Despite a hand injury from a prop bomb a few years before, he generally performed his own stunts.

Lloyd is widely considered to have been one of the three greatest comic actors of his time—the other two being Buster Keaton and Charlie Chaplin. But this is hard to quantify as he preferred not to re-release his early films after he finally retired from acting in the 1940s.

His chief attraction lay in the blithe way he got himself in and out of a huge variety of comic situations—all of them involving a high degree of physical danger, the more dangerous-looking the better. He was less deadpan than Keaton and far more "normal-looking" than Chaplin, so audiences found the characters he played relatively easy to identify with.

After 1929, Lloyd briefly made the transition to talkies (and was awarded a special Oscar in 1952 for his contribution to comedy), but he will always be associated with his many silent films, and with that dangerously mobile clock face.

MEL BROOKS'S SILENT MOVIE

Mel Brooks's main claim to fame these days is as the writer of *The Producers*—first the 1968 film and then the 21st-century stage musical. But way back in 1976, he wrote the screenplay for an (almost) silent movie—called *Silent Movie*.

The premise of the film is that Brooks and his friends want to make a movie but can only do so if various major stars (like Burt Reynolds, Liza Minnelli and Paul Newman) agree to take part. The irony is that the only word spoken during the whole film is when the French star Marcel Marceau (who built an entire career out of wordless mime) says: "Non!"

kings of comedy

> I gotta do some sad scenes. Why, I never tried to make anybody cry in my life! And I go 'round all the time dolled up in kippie clothes—wear everything but a corset! Can't stub my toe in this picture nor anything! Just imagine having to play-act all the time without ever getting hit with anything!
>
> Buster Keaton

THE FORGOTTEN CLOWN

At the height of his career he was considered equal to Charlie Chaplin, and yet silent movie star Harry Langdon has become the era's forgotten clown. His on screen persona—an innocent man-child, wearing a dented bowler hat, a tight jacket (with only the top button buttoned), a loosened tie and over-sized pants—reached its peak in the films of writer-director Frank Capra, but disappeared from the limelight with the arrival of screen sound.

But it wasn't simply the advent of sound that heralded the end for Langdon. The performer's nosedive in popularity coincided with artistic rifts with Capra, the genius behind Langdon's early fame. It seems that Langdon had begun to take the praise of his talent too seriously, and decided to go it alone, so that he could hog all the glory himself. His first solo film, the aptly name *Three's a Crowd,* was an artistic and commercial failure, the first of a series of filmatic flops that ruined Langdon's career and relegated him to minor films for the rest of his life.

The improbably named Roscoe Conkling Arbuckle (1887–1933), known professionally as "Fatty," was one of the highest-earning comedians of the silent movie era, earning $1 million a year from Paramount Studios—a staggering sum in the 1920s.

Like those in most silent movie comedies, his scenes were quick-moving, highly physical and full of stunts. He was also very fond of the traditional pie-in-the-face, although judging by his size, he must have eaten the mess between takes rather than wiped it off.

Arbuckle's relentless jollity came to an end when, in 1921, he was accused of raping and killing an actress, Virginia Rappe—an unfortunate surname in the circumstances. Miss Rappe died a few days after a drink-and-drug-fuelled party in the luxurious St Westin Hotel in San Francisco, and Fatty took the rap for the rape.

Despite medical evidence that the actress hadn't been assaulted, let alone raped, the local prosecutor decided to prosecute Arbuckle anyway, with lurid tales spreading of her being crushed by his weight.

Although the newspapers of the day revelled in the gory, rumored details, juries found little evidence that Arbuckle was in any way connected with her death. Yet Arbuckle endured not one but three trials.

Once his innocence was finally pronounced, the judge took the unheard-of step of issuing a written apology for his having been tried at all. But his career was ruined, by the scandal, if not the verdict.

Arbuckle died of heart failure in New York in 1933, his last years ruined and the light-hearted comedies that had made his name banned from publication after his disgrace. A real-life case of the tears of a clown.

Silent movies didn't do dialogue, but they did do music, in a big way, to provide atmosphere. Carl Davis, a leading contemporary composer, has led the way in writing scores for reissues of silent movie greats. Here are a few of the films he's brought back to life:

The Four Horsemen of the Apocalypse (1921)
One of Rudolph Valentino's greatest films

The Thief of Baghdad (1924)
Douglas Fairbanks swashbuckles stylishly

The Gold Rush (1925)
Chaplin comic classic

Ben Hur (1925)
The Ramon Novarro silent version

Flesh and the Devil (1926)
John Gilbert and Lars Hanson fall in love with Greta Garbo

Napoleon (1927)
French classic on Bonaparte's life

Failure is unimportant. It takes courage to make a fool of yourself.

Charlie Chaplin

CHARLIE CHAPLIN'S BIGGEST HITS

The Immigrant (1917)
A good example of Chaplin comedy, *The Immigrant* is most famous for the shot of the tramp and other immigrants as they lay their eyes on the Statue of Liberty for the first time.

The Kid (1921)
Chaplin's tramp finds a baby who grows into a kid (played by child star Jackie Coogan) and together they work various scams.

The Gold Rush (1925)
The tramp goes looking for gold in this silver-screen classic—at one point he hungrily tucks into his boot (times are hard) and his house slides down a hill. But then who ever laughed at good luck?

City Lights (1931)
One of Chaplin's best films (according to Woody Allen) and Orson Welles's favorite, this time featuring the tramp wooing a blind girl who mistakes him for a millionaire.

Limelight (1952)
Not a silent movie, but it has a wonderful wordless scene between two of the genre's greatest stars: Chaplin and Buster Keaton.

In a mere half century, films have gone from silent to unspeakable.

Doug Larson

> **If we don't change direction soon, we'll end up where we're going.**
>
> Professor Irwin Corey, US vaudeville comic and actor

SILENT SALARIES

Acting fees paid to Charlie Chaplin for his cinematic works:
$150/week
Caught in the Rain (1914)
Twenty Minutes of Love (1914)
Mabel's Strange Predicament (1914)
Kid Auto Races in Venice (1914)
Making a Living (1914)

Acting fees paid to Buster Keaton:
$1,500/week
Sunset Boulevard (1950)

$2,500/week
Love Nest on Wheels (1937)
Ditto (1937)
Jail Bait (1937)
Mixed Magic (1936)
The Chemist (1936)
Blue Blazes (1936)
Grand Slam Opera (1936)
Three on a Limb (1936)
The Timid Young Man (1935)
The E-Flat Man (1935)
Tars and Stripes (1935)
Hayseed Romance (1935)
One Run Elmer (1935)
Palooka from Paducah (1935)
(Source: www.imdb.com)

The final curtain

THE END

COMEDIANS WHO DIED TOO YOUNG

Richard Beckinsale (*Porridge*, *Rising Damp*) – **31**
Bill Hicks (American stand-up comedian) – **32**
John Belushi (*The Blues Brothers*) – **33**
Chris Farley (American comedian) – **33**
Mitch Hedberg (American comedian) – **37**
John Candy (American comedian) – **43**
James Beck (*Dad's Army*) – **44**
Dermot Morgan (*Father Ted*) – **45**
Carolyn Jones (*The Addams Family*) – **54**
Elizabeth Montgomery (*Bewitched*) – **62**

THE DEATH OF VICTOR MELDREW

One Foot in the Grave was a phenomenally successful BBC comedy about a miserable old man. Victor Meldrew (Richard Wilson), like the heroes of many British sitcoms, was a man at war with his circumstances, in this case old age and retirement. Audience sympathy was firmly with his long-suffering wife Margaret (Annette Crosbie).

In 2000, the plot took a turn unusual for any sitcom, however dark: the writers decided to kill off their main character. Accordingly, Victor was killed in a hit-and-run accident while making his way home from an unsuccessful school reunion (nobody showed up).

This was not the end of the show, however. A few weeks later, Meldrew pitched up as a ghost, ranting and raving at Margaret as though nothing had happened. It was only when he twigged that she could neither see nor hear him that he recognized his predicament.

He reacted with the catchphrase that British viewers had feared they would never hear again, an outraged: "I don't belieeeve it!"

Wilson couldn't hide his delight when the character was finally laid to rest, but he still has to endure shouts of: "I don't belieeeve it!" wherever he goes.

Here are the last utterances of eight comedians, plus one composer with the subject of comedy on the brain:

That was the best ice-cream soda I ever tasted
Lou Costello (d. 1959), half of the comedy team Abbott and Costello

Why not? After all, it belongs to him
Charlie Chaplin (d. 1977), after the priest giving him the last rites
had said "May God have mercy on your soul"

Friends applaud, the comedy is finished
Ludwig van Beethoven (d. 1827)

God damn the whole friggin' world and everyone in it but you, Carlotta!
W. C. Fields (d. 1946), to his mistress Carlotta Marti,
before he died on Christmas Day

I've said all I have to say
Bill Hicks (d. 1994). He made this announcement two weeks before his death,
but was as good as his (last) word

Yes it's tough, but not as tough as doing comedy
Edmund Gwenn (d. 1959) to Jack Lemmon, who had just asked him
whether dying was difficult

Do you know where I can get any s**t?
Lenny Bruce (d. 1966)

Surprise me
Bob Hope (d. 2003), the supposed reply to his son's question
about where he wanted to be buried

I must end it. There's no hope left. I'll be at peace.
No one had anything to do with this. My decision totally
Freddie Prinze (d. 1977), in his suicide note

Most familiar to viewers of the 1960s as their cloth-capped alter-egos Pete 'n' Dud, Peter Cook and Dudley Moore formed one of the most influential comedy duos in British television history. Cook was tall, fair and languid, whereas Moore was a short (5ft 2in), dark, working-class pianist with a club foot. But the two had a special chemistry, and their show *Not Only but Also* was compulsory viewing for a generation.

From the 1970s onwards, Moore's and Cook's careers took divergent paths. While Dudley Moore was making it big in Hollywood, Cook became increasingly withdrawn and dependent on the bottle. But the pair will always be united in the public imagination, not least because they both died tragically. Cook was the first to go. He died in 1995, aged 57, of internal haemorrhaging caused by excessive drinking. Moore was distraught, and called Cook's number several times over the next few weeks just to hear his voice on the answerphone.

In 1999, Moore announced that he had been diagnosed with Progressive Supranuclear Palsy, a condition considered incurable. Two years later, he displayed great courage when he travelled to Buckingham Palace to be invested as a CBE (Commander of the British Empire) in defiance of his deteriorating health. He died in 2002 aged 66.

LONG-LIVED COMEDIANS

George Burns (American comedian) – **100**
Bob Hope (American comedian) – **100**
Victor Borge (Danish comic pianist) – **91**
Durwood Kirby (American *Candid Camera* presenter) – **88**
Arnold Ridley (*Dad's Army*) – **88**
Bill Owen (*Last of the Summer Wine*) – **85**
Red Skelton (American TV clown) – **84**
John Laurie (*Dad's Army*) – **83**
Harold Bennett (*Are You Being Served?*) – **82**
Rodney Dangerfield (American stand-up comedian) – **82**

Kenny McCormick is a mumbling eight-year-old "hoody" who gets killed in (nearly) every episode of the R-rated cartoon show *South Park*. Here are a few of the ways in which Kenny "buys the farm":

Killed by a bear • Impaled on a flag pole • Attacked by mutant turkeys • Pulled into a giant fan by a magnet • Shot by police in Romania • Killed by Cartman • Spontaneously combusts during an intense planetarium show •

Decapitated by Ozzie Osborne • Strangled himself playing swing-ball (tetherball) • Deranged by Christina Aguilera hallucinations • Shot by an airport security guard after toe-clippers are found in his luggage

EMU AND THE TV AERIAL

Rod Hull was a gentle English comedian, with a savage emu puppet at the end of one arm, who died trying to fix a television aerial. The coroner attributed his death to a heart attack, but those familiar with Hull's act were more inclined to blame the emu.

Emu and Hull developed their unusual partnership in Australia during the 1960s, becoming huge stars in Britain in the following decade. In 1972, Emu secured immortality by eating the Queen Mother's floral bouquet at the Royal Variety Performance. The essence of the act was Emu's apparent complete autonomy. Talk-show host Michael Parkinson described the bird as the "dark side" of Hull, having been subjected to a brutal beak-attack on live television. Fellow guest Billy Connolly warned Emu that he'd break his neck if he tried the same trick with him.

In March 1999, 63-year-old Hull was watching the Champions League quarter-final between Manchester United and Inter Milan on television when the picture went fuzzy. He asked his son Oliver to keep an eye on the screen while he went onto the roof to adjust the aerial. Shortly afterwards there was a crash followed by a loud thud as Hull's body fell through the greenhouse.

One episode of the classic sitcom begins with Basil chatting blithely to a guest who earlier complained of feeling unwell. The man is lying in his bed and thoroughly unresponsive. Only gradually does it dawn on Fawlty that he must have died during the night. The stressed-out proprietor jumps to the conclusion that the culprit is food poisoning, in particular a kipper of dubious provenance that the deceased had for breakfast in the hotel dining room the day before.

When the doctor arrives to examine the corpse, Basil waits in agony, terrified that his trading license will be suspended as soon as the cause of death is established. The verdict that the man has actually died of a heart attack is the cue for hilarious and wonderfully inappropriate celebration. But the hotel staff still face a big dilemma—how are they to keep news of the demise from the other guests? The remainder of the episode supplies the predictable answer: not very well.

In 1999, John Cleese revealed he got the inspiration for "The Kipper and the Corpse" from a conversation with the manager of London's Savoy Hotel during the late 1970s. When the comedian asked the hotelier what he thought was the most difficult situation regularly encountered in his profession, he received the answer: "The death of a guest." When Cleese came to write the episode, he remembered his contact at the Savoy and named the corpse "Mr. Leeman" in his honor.

> **For three days after death, hair and fingernails continue to grow, but phone calls taper off.**
>
> Johnny Carson

GRAHAM CHAPMAN'S MEMORIAL SERVICE

When Monty Python's Graham Chapman died of cancer in 1989, his former colleagues elected to skip the funeral in order to keep the paparazzi away and give Chapman's family some privacy. They did, however, send a wreath in the shape of Terry Gilliam's giant stamping foot.

The Pythons got their chance to celebrate Chapman's life in a suitably anarchic and irreverent fashion two months later at a memorial service in St. Bartholomew's Hospital Great Hall in London. Hymns included Chapman's personal favorite "Jelusalem," and a Chinese version of "Jerusalem" in which all the Rs are replaced by Ls.

John Cleese, delivering the address, memorably kicked off by staking a claim to be the first person to say the "f" word at a memorial service. He then uttered the immortal words: "Graham Chapman is no more. He has gone to meet his maker. He has run down the curtain and joined the choir invisible . . . He is an ex-Python." Eric Idle also had a turn at the lectern, informing the congregation that Chapman had been worn down by Michael Palin's endless conversation and had, in his opinion, chosen to die so as not to have to listen to him any more.

Proceedings ended on positive note with a stirring rendition of "Always Look on the Bright Side of Life" from *The Life of Brian*.

I don't feel old.
I don't feel anything till noon.
That's when it's time for my nap.

Bob Hope in extreme old age

> ## John Le Mesurier wishes it to be known that he conked out on November 15th. He sadly misses his family and friends.
>
> *Dad's Army* star's self-penned *Times* obituary notice, 1983

DYING ON THE JOB

When comedians refer to "dying," they usually mean failure to get a laugh when performing. A few of them, however, have literally expired on stage:

Tommy Cooper
Suffered a fatal heart attack while performing on live television at Her Majesty's Theatre in London, in 1984. The audience laughed, thinking it was part of his act.

Irene Ryan (Granny in *The Beverley Hillbillies*)
Suffered a stroke on stage and died six weeks later.

Eric Morecombe
Suffered a fatal heart attack during a curtain call.

Harry Einstein (American radio comedian)
Died while performing at a party for Lucille Ball.

Dick Shawn (American Comedian)
Died during a stand-up gig at the University of California in San Diego.

Redd Foxx (American comedian)
The star of *Sanford and Son* died on set while filming his comeback show *The Royal Family.*

TOO DANGEROUS TO LIVE

Bill Hicks was a furiously dedicated comic who seemed to have been born with an inbuilt zeal for performance. Playing gigs from the age of 13, he would often burn the midnight oil writing and refining his ideas. In the company of his friend, Dwight Slade, he became his own courier service and cycled tapes of his acts out to agents. His parents had him psychoanalyzed at 17, to no discernible effect, for a little later he found a vent for his anger by forming the punk band, Stress. In 1980, he moved from Houston to Los Angeles and began to play Hollywood's Comedy Store. LA, it's fair to say, got to him—and its pleasures threatened to undo his ambitions: at one point, he drank $1,700 worth of booze in a month. However, by 26 he was teetotal and honing his reputation as an attack-dog who savaged sacred cows of the political right and left. In the early 90s came his albums, *Dangerous* and *Relentless*, and it seemed there was no stopping him.

But in 1993, he was diagnosed with pancreatic cancer. Those who witnessed the final stage of his career say that the illness gave his righteous ire renewed vigor. Cynthia True's biography, *American Scream*, says that he, "Performed with the freedom of a man with nothing to lose," and Hicks himself felt that, "The possibilities (creatively) seem limitless." He died in February 1994. We can only wonder what he may have contributed to humor had he lived.

HE'D MURDER TO GET AN AUDIENCE

The great music hall comedian Sir George Robey (1869-1954) found a novel way to publicize his show during a season in Swansea in Wales. He got hold of a mannequin and rowed out to sea with it, making sure that the boat was clearly visible to holidaymakers on the town's beach. Soon a violent quarrel appeared to break out between the vessel's occupants. When Robey grabbed an oar and slammed it into the dummy, there were screams from the shore and a flurry of boats was launched to investigate. "The excitement became frantic," he recalled with satisfaction. Then he drew out a revolver and pumped six bullets into his "companion." "It was a good stunt," Robey acknowledged. "When I stepped onto the stage that night I was received with cheers and loud cries of 'What have you done with the body George?'"

FOREVER YOUNG

Poignantly, for those of us who are exactly that age, Jack Benny claimed to be 39 until and beyond the point when he had actually lived for twice as long. In affectionate deference to this delusion, Frank Sinatra gave him two copies of *Life Begins at 40* for his 80th birthday.

SMITH AND JONES GRAVEYARD SKETCH

Former *Not the Nine O'Clock News* stars Griff Rhys Jones and Mel Smith later teamed up to make a comedy series entitled *Alas Smith and Jones*. One of the funniest (and most excruciating) sketches takes place in a graveyard.

Jones plays a priest whose efforts to conduct a dignified burial are continually frustrated by Smith's clumsy, grief-stricken mourner. The trouble begins when the latter, blubbing uncontrollably, whips out a handkerchief to dry his eyes. With this action he inadvertently sends something flying from his pocket into the grave. The remainder of the ceremony is dominated by Smith's ever more desperate attempts to retrieve it without anyone noticing. Before long, to the considerable chagrin of the priest and other mourners, he is on his knees and reaching down into the grave. Then, of course, he falls into it. An embarrassed Smith emerges holding what he was looking for: his car keys. Then there is a sickening crunch and one side of him drops several inches. As he tries to clamber out, it becomes clear that his foot has gone through the lid of the coffin, which is now attached to him like a giant shoe. Agony is piled upon agony.

The author once caused minor injuries to a Polish gentleman by reenacting this sketch at a party. The Pole laughed so much he fell off his chair.

> **I told you I was ill.**
> Spike Milligan's epitaph. To avoid offense to visitors to the graveyard, it was carved on his headstone in Gaelic.

I like my coffee like I like my women:
in a plastic cup.
Eddie Izzard

The Movie Makers: Charlie Chaplin, Denis Gifford
Cleese Encounters, Jonathan Margolis
Tragically I Was an Only Twin—The Complete Peter Cook,
edited by William Cook
A Liar's Autobiography, Graham Chapman
Stan, Fred Lawrence Guiles
Bob Hope: The Road Well-Traveled, Lawrence K. J. Quirk
Buster Keaton, Marion Meade
Keaton: The Man Who Wouldn't Lie Down, Tom Dardis
Strawberries and Cream, Harry Secombe
Peter Sellers, Alexander Walker
Swann's Way, Donald Swann
Swanson on Swanson: The Making of a Hollywood Legend, Gloria Swanson

INDEX

INDEX